Student Solutions Manual for

Statistical Methods for Psychology
Fourth Edition

David C. Howell
The University of Vermont

Duxbury Press
An Imprint of Wadsworth Publishing Company
I(T)P® An International Thomson Publishing Company

Belmont, CA • Albany, NY • Bonn • Boston • Cincinnati • Detroit • Johannesburg • London • Madrid
Melbourne • Mexico City • New York • Paris • San Francisco • Singapore • Tokyo • Toronto • Washington

Table of Contents

Solutions

Chapter	1	Basic Concepts.	1
Chapter	2	Describing and Exploring Data.	3
Chapter	3	The Normal Distribution.	14
Chapter	4	Sampling Distributions and Hypothesis Testing.	18
Chapter	5	Basic Concepts of Probability.	21
Chapter	6	Chi-Square.	25
Chapter	7	Hypothesis Tests Applied to Means.	33
Chapter	8	Power.	41
Chapter	9	Correlation and Regression.	47
Chapter	10	Alternative Correlational Techniques.	54
Chapter	11	Simple Analysis of Variance.	60
Chapter	12	Multiple Comparisons Among Treatment Means.	70
Chapter	13	Factorial Analysis of Variance.	78
Chapter	14	Repeated Measures Designs.	88
Chapter	15	Multiple Regression.	100
Chapter	16	Analysis of Variance and Covariance as General Linear Models.	106
Chapter	17	Log-Linear Analysis.	115
Chapter	18	Nonparametric and Distribution-Free Statistical Tests.	120

General Notes

This manual contains answers to most of the odd-numbered exercises in *Statistical Methods for Psychology*, Fourth Edition. These solutions were checked using a variety of calculators and computer software. Answers often differ (sometimes a surprising amount) depending on how many decimal places the calculator or program carries. It is important not to be too concerned about differences, especially ones in the second or third decimal place, which may be attributable to rounding (or the lack thereof) in intermediate steps.

Although I do not provide detailed answers to all discussion questions, for reasons given elsewhere, I have provided pointers for what I am seeking for many (though not all) of them. I hope that these will facilitate using these items as a basis of classroom discussion.

Copyright Information

COPYRIGHT © 1997 by Wadsworth Publishing Company
A Division of International Thomson Publishing Inc.
I(T)P The ITP logo is a registered trademark under license.
Duxbury Press and the leaf logo are trademarks used under license.

Printed in the United States of America
1 2 3 4 5 6 7 8 9 10

ISBN 0-534-51999-7

Chapter 1 - Basic Concepts

1.1 The entire student body of your college or university would be considered a population under any circumstances in which you want to generalize *only* to the student body of your college or university and no further.

> You need to keep in mind that a population is the larger group about which you wish to make some statement. A sample is a subset of the population that is used to help you *estimate* characteristics of the sample. If you are looking at all the people or objects about which you are interested, then you have a population.

1.3 The students of your college or university are a nonrandom sample of U.S. students, for example, because all U.S. students do not have an equal chance of being included in the sample.

1.5 Independent variables: (a) First grade students who attended Kindergarten versus those who did not. (b) Seniors, Masters, Submasters, and Juniors as categories of marathon runners. Dependent variables: (a) Social-adjustment scores assigned by first-grade teachers. (b) Time to run 26 miles, 385 yards.

> Remember that Dependent and Data both start with a "D." Also remember that the independent variable is the one you change to see what happens to values of the dependent variable.

1.7 Continuous variables: (a) Length of gestation. (b) Typing speed in words/minute. (c) Level of serotonin in a particular subcortical nucleus.

1.9 The planners of a marathon race would like to know the average times of Senior, Master, Submaster, and Junior runners so as to facilitate planning for handling the finish line.

1.11 Categorical data: (a) The number of Brown University students in an October, 1984, referendum voting For and the number voting Against the university's stockpiling suicide pills in case of nuclear disaster. (b) The number of students in a small midwestern college who are White, Black, Latino, Asian, Native American, or Other. (c) One year after an experimental program to treat alcoholism, the number of participants who are "still on the wagon", "drinking without having sought treatment", or "again under treatment".

1.13 Children's scores in an inner-city elementary school could be reported numerically (a measurement variable), or the children could be categorized as Bluebirds ($X > 90$), Robins ($X = 70-90$), or Cardinals ($X > 70$).

1.15 For adults of a given height and sex, weight is a ratio scale of body weight, but it is *at best* an ordinal scale of physical health.

> The point of this exercise was to remind you that it is important to think about what the dependent variable is actually measuring. Just giving it a name is not enough.

1.17 Speed is probably a much better index of motivation than of learning.

1.19 (a) The final grade point averages for low-achieving students taking courses that interested them could be compared with the averages of low-achieving students taking courses which don't interest them. (b) The quality of communication could be compared for happily versus unhappily married couples.

Chapter 2 - Describing and Exploring Data

2.1   Children's recall of stories:

a.

Children's "and then...s"	Frequency
10	1
11	1
12	1
15	3
16	4
17	6
18	10
19	7
20	7
21	3
22	2
23	2
24	1
31	1
40	1

b. unimodal and positively skewed

2.3   The problem with making a stem-and-leaf display of the data in Exercise 2.1 is that almost all the values fall on only two leaves if we use the usual 10s' digits for stems.

Stem Leaf
```
1    012555566667777778888888889999999
2    000000011122334
3    1
4    0
```

And things aren't much better even if we double the number of stems.

Stem Leaf
```
1*      012
1.      5556666777777888888888889999999
2*      000000011122334
2.
3*      1
3.
4*      0
```

Best might be to use the units digits for stems and add HI and LO for extreme values:

Stem	Leaf
LO	0 1 2
5	555
6	6666
7	7777777
8	8888888888
9	9999999
10	0000000
11	111
12	22
13	33
14	4
HI	31 40

> Remember that stem-and-leaf displays were designed for your convenience.
> You can alter them in any way that makes sense to you, just so long as they
> are clear to other people who will look at them.

2.5 Stem-and-leaf diagram of the data in Exercises 2.1 and 2.4:

Children		Adults
	0*	1
	0t	34
	0f	55
	0s	7777
	0.	88889999999
10	1*	00000000111111
2	1t	222223
555	1f	4444555
7777776666	1s	667
77777778888888888	1.	
1110000000	2*	
3322	2t	
4	2f	
	2s	
	2.	
40 31	Hi	

4

2.7 Cumulative frequency distribution for data in Exercise 2-4:

Adult Scores	Frequency	Cumul. Frequency
1	1	1
3	1	2
4	1	3
5	2	5
7	4	9
8	4	13
9	7	20
10	8	28
11	6	34
12	5	39
13	1	40
14	4	44
15	3	47
16	2	49
17	1	50

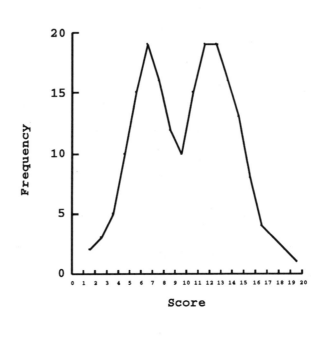

I omitted mention of cumulative distributions from this edition of the text, but forgot to remove the exercises on them. You should be able to tell from the plot in Exercise 12.7 what a cumulative distribution is. My apologies.

2.9 Invented bimodal data:

Score	Freq
1	2
2	3
3	5
4	10
5	15
6	19
7	16
8	12
9	10
10	15
11	19
12	19
13	16
14	13
15	8
16	4
17	3
18	2
19	1
20	1

2.11 Computer printout [Compare histogram to Exercise 2.4.]

2.13 Histogram for GPA:

GPA	Mid	Frequen
.51–.75	.63	4
.76–1.00	.88	5
1.01–1.25	1.13	1
1.26–1.50	1.38	6
1.51–1.75	1.63	7
1.76–2.00	1.88	6
2.01–2.25	2.13	6
2.26–2.50	2.38	8
2.51–2.75	2.63	14
2.76–3.00	2.88	13
3.01–3.25	3.13	3
3.26–3.50	3.38	7
3.51–3.75	3.63	6
3.76–4.00	3.88	2

2.15 **(1)** Mexico has very many young people and very few old people, while Spain has a more even distribution. **(2)** The difference between males and females is more pronounced at most ages in Spain than it is in Mexico. **(3)** You can see the high infant mortality rate in Mexico.

2.17 a. $Y_1 = 9 \quad Y_{10} = 2$

b. $\Sigma Y = 9 + 9 + \ldots + 2 = 57$

2.19 a. $(\Sigma Y)^2 = (9 + 9 + \ldots + 2)^2 = 3249$

$\Sigma Y^2 = 9^2 + 9^2 + \ldots + 2^2 = 377$

b.

$$\frac{\Sigma Y^2 - \dfrac{(\Sigma Y)^2}{N}}{N-1} = \frac{377 - \dfrac{3249}{10}}{9} = 5.789$$

c. $\sqrt{\text{answer to Exercise 2.19b}} = \sqrt{5.789} = 2.406$

d. The units of measurement were squared musicality scores in Exercise 2.19b and musicality scores in Exercise 2.19c.

2.21 a. $\Sigma(X + Y) = (10 + 9) + (8 + 9) + \ldots + (7 + 2) = 19 + 17 + \ldots + 9 = 134$

$\Sigma X + \Sigma Y = 77 + 57 = 134$

$\Sigma(X + Y) = 134 = \Sigma X + \Sigma Y$

b. $\Sigma XY = 10(9) + 8(9) + \ldots + 7(2) = 460$

$\Sigma X \Sigma Y = (77)(57) = 4389$

$\Sigma XY = 460 \neq 4389 = \Sigma X \Sigma Y$

c. $\Sigma CX = \Sigma 3X = 3(10) + 3(8) + \ldots + 3(7) = 231$

$C\Sigma X = 3(77) = 231$

$\Sigma CX = 231 = C\Sigma X$

d. $\Sigma X^2 = 10^2 + 8^2 + \ldots + 7^2 = 657$

$(\Sigma X)^2 = 77^2 = 5929$

$\Sigma X^2 = 657 \neq 5929 = (\Sigma X)^2$

2.23 Stem-and-leaf displays:

	1 Stimulus		3 Stimuli		5 Stimuli
3.	678899	3.		3.	9
4*	11122333344444	4*	23	4*	
4.	5555556666667777777889999	4.	666779	4.	6689
5*	111122222333444	5*	0011111112222222333333344	5*	13344
5.	566677778899	5.	5566666788889999999	5.	5555566778888899
6*	1124	6*	000000011111222222233333333444	6*	1111222222333444
6.	6777	6.	5566777799	6.	555555566667777777788999999
7*	112234	7*	22223344	7*	1122444
7.	69	7.	58	7.	566677889
8*		8*	3	8*	11233
8.		8.	6	8.	578
9*	4	9*		9*	4
9.		9.	5	9.	58
10*	44	10*		10*	
10.		10.		10.	
11*		11.		11*	
11.		11*		11.	
12*		12.		12*	
12.		12*		12.	5

As the number of digits in the comparison stimulus increases, the response time increases as well.

2.25 You could compare the reaction times for those cases in which the correct response was "Yes" and those cases in which it was "No." If we process information sequentially, the reaction times, on average, should be longer for the "No" condition than for the "Yes" condition because we would have to make comparisons against all stimuli in the comparison set. In the "Yes" condition we could stop as soon as we found a match.

> This experiment by Sternberg is actually a classic experiment investigating information processing. It appears in many introductory texts, and illustrates how a very simple experiment will tell us a great deal about internal processes.

2.27 For animals raised in a stable environment, there is little or no difference in immunity depending on Affiliation. However, for animals raised in an unstable environment, High Affiliation subjects showed much greater immunity than Low Affiliation subjects. Stability seems to protect against the negative effects of low affiliation.

> Keep in mind that we have not yet shown that this phenomenon is reliable. We will discuss how to do that in Chapter 13. In this case, reliability refers to our expectation of whether we would find such differences if we reran the experiment one or more times. In fact, I know from other sources that the difference in the effect of affiliation in stable and unstable environments is reliable.

2.29 There are any number of ways that these data could be plotted. Perhaps the simplest is to look at the change in the *percentages* of each ethnic group's representation from 1982 to 1991.

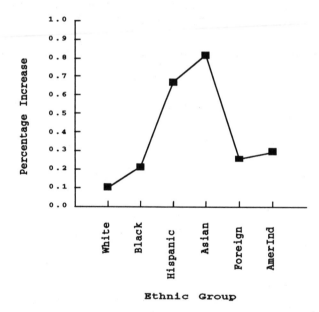

Change in Ethnic Distribution in U.S. Colleges

2.31 One way to look at these data is to plot the percentage of households headed by women and the family size separately against years. Notice that there is an uneven sampling of years.

Percent Households Headed by Women

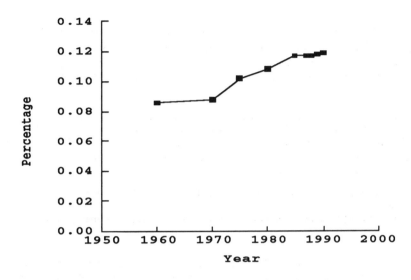

a. There has been a dramatic increase in the percentage of households headed by women over the past 10 years.

b. There has also been a corresponding decrease in family size, part of which is perhaps due to the increase in single-parent families.

Family Size Decreases Over Time

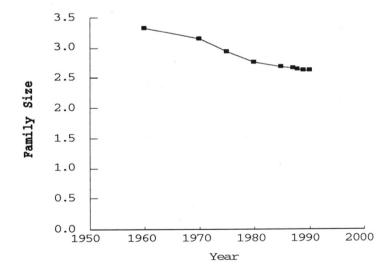

2.33 The mean falls above the median.

2.35 Rats running a straight alley maze:

$$\overline{X} = \frac{\Sigma X}{N} = \frac{320}{15} = 21.33; \text{Median} = 21$$

> When our data are grouped, as they are here, we obtain the total simply by multiplying each score by its frequency, and summing the results. The mean is then just the total divided by the number of observations.

2.37 Multiplying by a constant:

Original data (X):	8	3	5	5	6	2	$\overline{Y} = 4.83$
							Median = 5
							Mode = 5
Transformed data (Y = 3X):	24	9	15	15	18	6	$\overline{Y} = 14.5$
							Median = 15
							Mode = 15

$$3\,\overline{X} = \overline{Y} \qquad\qquad 3(\text{Med}_x) = \text{Med}_y \qquad\qquad 3(\text{Mo}_x) = \text{Mo}_y$$
$$3(4.83) = 14.5 \qquad\qquad 3(5) = 15 \qquad\qquad 3(5) = 15$$
$$14.5 = 14.5 \qquad\qquad 15 = 15 \qquad\qquad 15 = 15$$

2.39 Computer printout   [Compare answers to Exercise 2.22]

2.41 The distribution of GPA is somewhat asymmetric, with Bs and Cs predominating. There were a few students with an A average, but none who failed all of their courses.

2.43 For the data in Exercise 2.4:

$$\text{range} = 17 - 1 = 16$$

$$\text{variance} = s_x^2 = \frac{\Sigma X^2 - \frac{(\Sigma X)^2}{N}}{N-1} = \frac{5770 - \frac{510^2}{50}}{49} = 11.592$$

$$\text{standard deviation} = s_x = \sqrt{s_x^2} = \sqrt{11.592} = 3.405$$

2.45 For the data in Exercise 2.1:

The interval: $\overline{X} \pm 2s_x = 18.9 \pm 2(4.496) = 18.9 \pm 8.992 = 9.908 \text{ to } 27.892$

From the frequency distribution in Exercise 2.1 we can see that all but two scores (31 and 40) fall in this interval, therefore 48/50 = 96% of the scores fall in this interval.

2.47 Original data: 2   3   4   4   5   5   9 $\overline{X}_1 = 4.57$ $s_1 = 2.23$
(reordered)

$X_2 = X_1 + 3$:   5   6   7   7   8   8   12 $\overline{X}_2 = 7.57$ $s_2 = 2.23$

$X_3 = X_1 - 2$:   0   1   2   2   3   3   7 $\overline{X}_3 = 2.57$ $s_3 = 2.23$

$$\overline{X}_1 = \frac{32}{7} = 4.57 \qquad \overline{X}_2 = \frac{53}{7} = \overline{X}_1 + 3 \qquad \overline{X}_3 = \frac{18}{7} = 2.57 = \overline{X}_1 - 2$$

$$s_1 = \sqrt{\frac{\Sigma X_1^2 - \dfrac{(\Sigma X_1)^2}{N}}{N-1}} \qquad s_2 = \sqrt{\frac{\Sigma X_2^2 - \dfrac{(\Sigma X_2)^2}{N}}{N-1}} \qquad s_3 = \sqrt{\frac{\Sigma X_3^2 - \dfrac{(\Sigma X_3)^2}{N}}{N-1}}$$

$$= \sqrt{\frac{176 - \dfrac{32^2}{7}}{6}} \qquad\qquad = \sqrt{\frac{431 - \dfrac{53^2}{7}}{6}} \qquad\qquad = \sqrt{\frac{76 - \dfrac{18^2}{7}}{6}}$$

$$= 2.23 \qquad\qquad\qquad = 2.23 \qquad\qquad\qquad = 2.23$$

As we saw in Exercise 2.22, adding (or subtracting) a constant to (or from) a distribution adds (or subtracts) that constant from the mean of that distribution. Here we find that the standard deviation of that distribution is unchanged.

2.49 Original data: 5   8   3   8   6   9   9   7

$$s_1 = \sqrt{\frac{409 - \dfrac{55^2}{8}}{7}} = \sqrt{4.411} = 2.1$$

If $X_2 = CX_1$, then $s_2 = Cs_1$ and we want $s_2 = 1.00$

$$s_2 = Cs_1$$
$$1 = C(2.1)$$
$$\frac{1}{2.1} = C$$

Therefore we want to divide the original scores by 2.1

$$X_2 = \frac{X_1}{2.1}: \quad 2.381 \quad 3.809 \quad 1.428 \quad 3.809 \quad 2.857 \quad 4.286 \quad 4.286 \quad 3.333$$

$$s_2 = \sqrt{\frac{92.736 - \frac{26.19^2}{8}}{7}} = \sqrt{\frac{6.9965}{7}} = \sqrt{1} = 1$$

> In this example we rely on the fact that dividing a set of data by a constant divides the standard deviation by that constant. So, we first found the standard deviation. Since we want to reduce the new standard deviation to 1 (= s.d./s.d.), we just divide the whole distribution by the size of the standard deviation.

2.51 Boxplot for the data in Exercise 2.1 [Refer to data in Exercise 2.1 and cumulative distribution in Exercise 2.6]:

Median location = $(N + 1)/2 = 51/2 = 25.5$
Median = 18
Hinge location = (Median location + 1)/2 = $(25 + 1)/2 = 26/2 = 13$
Hinges = 17 and 20
H-spread = 20 - 17 = 3
Inner fences = Hinges ± 1.5(H − spread)

$$= 17 - 1.5(3) = 17 - 4.5 = 12.5$$

$$and = 20 + 1.5(3) = 20 + 4.5 = 24.5$$
Adjacent values = 15 and 24

```
        0    5   10   15   20   25   30   35   40   45   50
        +----+----+----+----+----+----+----+----+----+----+

              ***   --||  |----        *          *
```

2.53 Boxplot for ADDSC [Refer to stem-and-leaf in Exercise 2.15]:

Median location = $(N + 1)/2 = (88 + 1)/2 = 89/2 = 44.5$
Median = 50
Hinge location = (Median location + 1)/2 = $(44 + 1)/2 = 45/2 = 22.5$
Hinges = 44.5 and 60.5
H-spread = 60.5 - 44.5 = 16
Inner fences = Hinges ± 1.5(H − spread)

$$= 60.5 + 1.5(16) = 60.5 + 24 = 84.5$$

$$and = 44.5 - 1.5(16) = 44.5 - 24 = 20.5$$
Adjacent values = 26 and 78

12

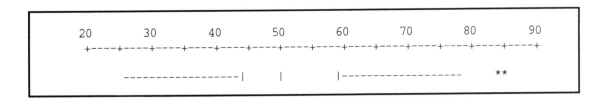

```
        20        30        40        50        60        70        80        90
        +----+----+----+----+----+----+----+----+----+----+----+----+----+----+
              ----------------|     |    |----------------      **
```

2.55 Coefficient of variation for Appendix Data Set:

$$s / \overline{X} = 0.8614 / 2.456 = 0.351$$

Execustat gave an answer of 35.071 because it multiplied by 100 to present the coefficient of variation of the standard deviation as a *percentage* of the mean.

2.57 There are a number of problems with the report of these data and their interpretation. I am impressed with the way the student approached the problem and what she had to say about her results. I am not impressed with the way the media reported the data, because some of their statements cannot possibly be true. I also think that they are placing a lot of faith in the reporting of the subjects.

Chapter 3 - Normal Distribution

3.1 **a.** Original data:

1   2   2   3   3   3   4   4   4   4   5   5   5   6   6   7

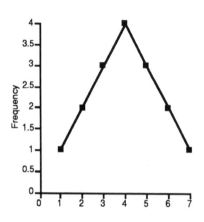

b. To convert the distribution to a distribution of X - μ, subtract
μ = 4 from each score:

-3   -2   -2   -1   -1   -1   0   0   0   0   1   1   1   2   2   3

c. To complete the conversion to z, divide each score by σ = 1.63:

-1.84   -1.23   -1.23   -0.61   -0.61   -0.61   0   0   0   0
0.61   0.61   0.61   1.23   1.23   1.84

> This is just the continuation of the material you saw in the last chapter
> about what happens to the mean and standard deviation when you add,
> subtract, multiply, and divide by a constant. You may not think that you
> will do this very much, but you do it in subtle ways when you omit
> decimal points, scale data, or put two or more sets of data on a common
> base.

3.3 Errors counting shoppers in a major department store:

a.
$$z = \frac{X - \mu}{\sigma}$$

$$= \frac{960 - 975}{15} = -\frac{15}{15} = -1 \qquad \text{between -1 and μ lie .3413}$$

$$= \frac{990 - 975}{15} = +\frac{15}{15} = +1 \qquad \text{between +1 and μ lie } \underline{.3413}$$

$$.6826$$

Therefore between 960 and 990 are found approximately 68% of the scores.

14

b. $975 = \mu$; therefore 50% of the scores lie below 975.

c.   .5000 lie below 975
       <u>.3413</u> lie between 975 and 990
       .8413 (or 84%) lie below 990

3.5   The supervisor's count of shoppers:

$$z = \frac{X - \mu}{\sigma}$$

$$= \frac{950 - 975}{15}$$

$$= -1.67 \qquad \text{X to} \pm 1.67 = 2(.0475) = .095; \text{ therefore 9.5% of the time scores}$$

will be at least this extreme.

3.7   They would be equal when the two distributions have the same standard deviation.

3.9   Next year's salary raises:

a.
$$z = \frac{X - \mu}{\sigma}$$

$$-1.2817 = \frac{X - 2000}{400}$$

$$\$2512.68 = X$$

10% of the faculty will have a raise equal to or greater than \$2512.68.

b.
$$z = \frac{X - \mu}{\sigma}$$

$$-1.645 = \frac{X - 2000}{400}$$

$$\$1342 = X$$

The 5% of the faculty who haven't done anything useful in years will receive no more than \$1342 each, and probably don't deserve that much.

3.11 Transforming scores on diagnostic test for language problems:

X_1 = original scores $\qquad \mu_1 = 48 \qquad \sigma_1 = 7$

X_2 = transformed scores $\qquad \mu_2 = 80 \qquad \sigma_2 = 10$

$\sigma_2 = \sigma_1 / C$

$10 = 7 / C$

$C = .7$

Therefore to transform the original standard deviation from 7 to 10, we need to divide the original scores by .7. However dividing the original scores by .7 divides their mean by .7.

$$\overline{X}_2 = \overline{X}_1 / .7 = 48 / .7 = 68.57$$

We want to raise the mean to 80. $80 - 68.57 = 11.43$. Therefore we need to add 11.43 to each score.

$X_2 = X_1 / .7 + 11.43$ [This formula summarizes the whole process.]

3.13 October 1981 GRE, all people taking exam:

$$z = \frac{X - \mu}{\sigma}$$

$$= \frac{600 - 489}{126}$$

$$= .88 \quad p(\text{larger portion}) = .81$$

A GRE score of 600 would correspond to the 81st percentile.

3.15 October 1981 GRE, all seniors and nonenrolled college graduates:

$$z = \frac{X - \mu}{\sigma} \qquad\qquad z = \frac{X - \mu}{\sigma}$$

$$= \frac{600 - 507}{118} \qquad\qquad .6745 = \frac{X - 507}{118}$$

$$= .79 \quad p = .785 \qquad\qquad 586.591 = X$$

For seniors and nonenrolled college graduates, a GRE score of 600 is at the 79th percentile, and a score of 587 would correspond to the 75th percentile.

3.17 GPA scores: $N = 88$ $\overline{X} = 2.46$ $s = .86$ [calculated from data set]

$$z = \frac{X - \overline{X}}{s}$$

$$.6745 = \frac{X - 2.46}{.86}$$

$$3.04 = X$$

The 75th percentile for GPA is 3.04.

3.19 There is no meaningful discrimination to be made among those scoring below the mean, and therefore all people who score in that range are given a T score of 50.

> You might well ask why those scores are called T scores if they have such a strange distribution. And that would be a good question. The point is that they really can be thought of as T scores for higher values, and they are used as such. But they are definitely misleading for low values.

Chapter 4 - Hypothesis Testing

4.1   Was last night's game an NHL hockey game?

   a. Null hypothesis: The game was actually an NHL hockey game.

   b. On the basis of that null hypothesis I expected that each team would earn somewhere between 0 and 6 points. I then looked at the actual points and concluded that they were way out of line with what I would expect if this were an NHL hockey game. I therefore rejected the null hypothesis.

> The point here is that the logic of hypothesis testing really comes down to laying out (or calculating) what you would expect if the null hypothesis were true, and then looking to see if the results are consistent with that expectation.

4.3   A Type I error would be concluding that I had been shortchanged when in fact I had not.

> Remember that a Type I error is one of rejecting a null hypothesis when it is in fact true, whereas a Type II error is failing to reject it when it is false. If the null hypothesis is that I was charged correctly, and if I really was charged correctly, then claiming to be short changed would be a Type I error (and would also be very embarrassing,)

4.5   The critical value would be that amount of change below which I would decide that I had been shortchanged. The rejection region would be all amounts less than the critical value—i.e., all amounts that would lead to rejection of H_0.

4.7   Was the son of the member of the Board of Trustees fairly admitted to graduate school?

$$\overline{X} = 650 \quad s = 50$$

$$z = \frac{490 - 650}{50}$$

$$= -3.2$$

z score	p
3.00	0.0013
3.20	0.0007
3.25	0.0006

The probability that a student drawn at random from those properly admitted would have a GRE score as low as 490 is .0007. I suspect that the fact that his mother was a member of the Board of Trustees played a role in his admission.

4.9   The distribution would drop away smoothly to the right for the same reason that it always does—there are few high-scoring people. It would drop away steeply to the left because fewer of the borderline students would be admitted (however high the borderline is set).

> Data which come about as a result of some sort of cutoff (even if it is not a tightly fixed cutoff) often have skewed distributions.

4.11 M is called a test statistic.

4.13 The alternative hypothesis is that this student was sampled from a population of students whose mean is not equal to 650.

4.15 The word "distribution" refers to the set of values obtained for any set of observations. The phrase "sampling distribution" is reserved for the distribution of outcomes (either theoretical or empirical) of a sample statistic.

> Whenever you are looking at the distribution of some statistic, you are looking at a sampling distribution.

4.17 **a.** *Research hypothesis—Children* who attend kindergarten adjust to 1st grade faster than those who do not. *Null hypothesis—*1st-grade adjustment rates are equal for children who did and did not attend Kindergarten.

b. *Research hypothesis—*Sex education in junior high school decreases the rate of pregnancies among unmarried mothers in high school. *Null hypothesis—*The rate of pregnancies among unmarried mothers in high school is the same regardless of the presence or absence of sex education in junior high school.

4.19 Finger-tapping cutoff if $\alpha = .01$:

$$z = \frac{X - \mu}{\sigma}$$

$$-2.327 = \frac{X - 100}{20}$$

z score	p
2.3200	0.9898
2.3270	0.9900
2.3300	0.9901

$$53.46 = X$$

For α to equal .01, z must be -2.327. The cutoff score is therefore 53. The corresponding value for z when a cutoff score of 53 is applied to the curve for H_1:

$$z = \frac{X - \mu}{\sigma}$$

$$= \frac{53.46 - 80}{20}$$

$$= -1.33$$

Looking $z = -1.33$ up in Appendix z, we find that .9082 of the scores fall above a score of 53.46. β is therefore 0.908.

4.21 To determine whether there is a true relationship between grades and course evaluations I would find a statistic that reflected the degree of relationship between two variables. (The students will see such a statistic (r) in the Chapter 9.) I would then calculate the sampling distribution of that statistic in a situation in which there is no relationship between two variables. Finally, I would calculate the statistic for a representative set of students and classes and compare my sample value with the sampling distribution of that statistic.

4.23 Computer exercise. The distribution of the raw data will not be completely flat because of sampling error and any error in the random number generator (which will never be perfect).

4.25 **c.** This is an interesting problem. On the one hand they have all of the states, so they have the parameters and don't have to estimate them. On the other hand, it would be interesting to test a general hypothesis about whether there is something about private ownership that keeps prices up (or down). I just don't see how you test that here. Students may struggle with this one.

> I think that part of the problem that I have is that the question keeps changing in my mind. If I want to really know if "monopoly" states have a lower mean price than "non-monopoly" states, I just need to look at the means. A one cent difference is still a difference. But I think my question really is more about whether there is something about being a monopoly state that gives a lower mean, and that question may not be answerable by these data. Just because I wrote the questions doesn't mean that I know all the answers.

Chapter 5 - Basic Concepts of Probability

5.1 **a.** Analytic: If two tennis players are exactly equally skillful so that the outcome of their match is random, the probability is .50 that Player A will win the upcoming match.

   b. Relative frequency: If in past matches Player A has beaten Player B on 13 of the 17 occasions on which they played, then Player A has a probability of 13/17 = .76 of winning their upcoming match, all other things held constant.

   c. Subjective: Player A's coach feels that he has a probability of .90 of winning his upcoming match with Player B.

5.3 **a.** p(that you will win 2nd prize given that you don't win 1st) = 1/9 = .111

   b. p(that he will win 1st and you 2nd) = (2/10)(1/9) = (.20)(.111) = .022

   c. p(that you will win 1st and he 2nd) = (1/10)(2/9) = (.10)(.22) = .022

   d. p(that you are 1st and he 2nd [= .022]) + p(that he is 1st and you 2nd [= .022]) = p(that you and he will be 1st and 2nd) = .044.

   > Many problems in probability, such as this one, can often be solved by simply enumerating the possible outcomes.

5.5 Conditional probabilities were involved in Exercise 5.3a.

5.7 Conditional probabilities: What is the probability that skiing conditions will be good on Wednesday, *given* that they are good today?

   > As a general rule of thumb, you are talking about conditional probabilities whenever the word "given," or "when," or their equivalent is used.

5.9 p(that they will look at each other at the same time during waking hours) = p(that mother looks at baby during waking hours) * p(that baby looks at mother during waking hours) = (2/13)(3/13) = (.154)(.231) = .036

5.11 A continuous distribution for which we care about the probability of an observation's falling within some specified interval is exemplified by the probability that your baby will be born on its due date.

5.13 Two examples of discrete variables: Variety of meat served at dinner tonight; Brand of microcomputer owned.

5.15 **a.** 20%, or 60 applicants, will fall at or above the 80th percentile and 10 of these will be chosen. Therefore p(that an applicant with the highest rating will be admitted) = 10/60 = .167.

   b. No one below the 80th percentile will be admitted, therefore p(that an applicant with the lowest rating will be admitted) = 0/300 = .00.

5.17 Mean ADDSC score for boys = 54.29, s = 12.90   [Calculated from Data Set]

    a. Since a score of 50 is below the mean, and since we are looking for the probability of a score *greater than* 50, we want to look in the tables of the normal distribution in the column labeled "larger portion".

    p(larger portion) = .6293

    b. (Notice that one percentage refers to the proportion *greater than* 50, while the other refers to the proportion *greater than or equal to* 50.)

5.19 Compare the probability of dropping out of school, ignoring the ADDSC score, with the conditional probability of dropping out given that ADDSC in elementary school exceeded some value (e.g., 66).

5.21 Plot of correct choices on trial 1 of a 5-choice task:

p(0) = .1074
p(1) = .2684
p(2) = .3020
p(3) = .2013
p(4) = .0881
p(5) = .0264
p(6) = .0055
p(7) = .0008
p(8) = .0001
p(9) = .0000
p(10) = .0000

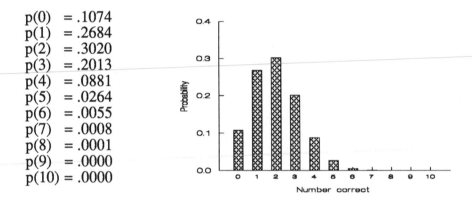

> Notice that this distribution is skewed. It will always be skewed unless the probabilities of success and failure are both .50. It will become more skewed as *p* and *q* depart more and more from 50:50.

5.23

$$p(\text{5 or more correct}) = p(5) + p(6) + p(7) + p(8) + p(9) + p(10)$$
$$= .0264 + .0055 + .0008 + .0001 + .0000 + .0000$$
$$= .028 < .05$$

$$p(\text{4 or more correct}) = p(4) + p(5) + p(6) + p(7) + p(8) + p(9) + p(10)$$
$$= .0881 + .0264 + .0055 + .0008 + .0001 + .0000 + .0000$$
$$= .1209 > .05$$

At $\alpha = .05$, therefore, up to 4 correct choices indicate chance performance, but 5 or more correct choices would lead me to conclude that they are no longer performing at chance levels.

> Here you have to look for the highest (or lowest, depending on the problem) value of an event that has a cumulative probability less than α, which, in this book, is .05.

5.25   If there is no housing discrimination, then a person's race and whether or not they are offered a particular unit of housing are independent events. We could calculate the probability that a particular unit (or a unit in a particular section of the city) will be offered to anyone in a specific income group. We can also calculate the probability that the customer is a member of an ethnic minority. We can then calculate the probability of that person being shown the unit assuming independence and compare that answer against the actual proportion of times a member of an ethnic minority was offered such a unit.

5.27   Number of subjects needed in Exercise 5.26's verbal learning experiment if each subject can see only two of the four classes of words:

$$P_2^4 = \frac{4!}{(4-2)!} = \frac{4!}{2!} = 12$$

5.29   The total number of ways of making ice cream cones =

$$C_6^6 + C_5^6 + C_4^6 + C_3^6 + C_2^6 + C_1^6 = 1 + 6 + 15 + 20 + 15 + 6 = 63$$

[You can't have an ice cream cone without ice cream; exclude C_0^6.]

5.31   Knowledge of current events:

If $p = .50$ of being correct on any one true-false item, and $N = 20$:

$$p(11) = (C_{11}^{20}) \times 5^{11} \times 5^9$$

$$C_{11}^{20} = \frac{20!}{11!(20-11)!} = \frac{20!}{11!9!} = 167,960$$

$$p(11) = (C_{11}^{20}) \times 5^{11} \times 5^9 = 167,960(.00048828)(.00195313) = .16$$

Since the probability of 11 correct by chance is .16, the probability of 11 <u>or more</u> correct must be greater than .16. Therefore we can not reject the hypothesis that $p = .50$ (student is guessing) at $\alpha = .05$.

5.33   On the theory that practice in almost anything leads to improvement, we give a sample of first year college students, who will major in the humanities (where there is a lot of reading assigned), a test for reading speed at the beginning of the fall semester. At the end of the year we again measure their reading speed. We wish to test the null hypothesis that reading speed, on average (or for most people) increased over the year.

Chapter 6 - Chi-Square

6.1   Popularity of psychology professors:

	Anderson	Klatsky	Kamm	Total
Observed	32	25	10	67
Expected	22.3	22.3	22.3	67

$$\chi^2 = \Sigma \frac{(O-E)^2}{E}$$

$$= \frac{(32-22.3)^2}{22.3} + \frac{(25-22.3)^2}{22.3} + \frac{(10-22.3)^2}{22.3}$$

$$= 11.33^1 \quad [\chi^2_{.05(2)} = 5.99]$$

Reject H_0 and conclude that students do not enroll at random.

> In this question our expected frequencies come from just assuming that the students would be evenly distributed across the classes if there were no preference.

6.3   Sorting one-sentence characteristics into piles:

	1	2	3	4	5	Total
Observed	8	10	20	8	4	50
Expected	5	10	20	10	5	50
Exp. %	10%	20%	40%	20%	10%	100%

$$\chi^2 = \Sigma \frac{(O-E)^2}{E}$$

$$= \frac{(8-5)^2}{5} + \frac{(10-10)^2}{10} + \frac{(20-20)^2}{20} + \frac{(8-10)^2}{10} + \frac{(4-5)^2}{5}$$

$$= 2.4 \quad [\chi^2_{.05(4)} = 9.49]$$

---

[1]The answers to these problems may differ substantially depending on the number of decimal places that are carried for the expected frequencies. (E.g. for Exercise 6.18, answers can vary between 37.141 and 37.229.)

Do not reject H_0 that your friend's child's sorting behavior is in line with your theory.

6.5 Racial choice in dolls (Clark & Clark, 1939):

	Black	White	Total
Observed	83	169	252
Expected	126	126	252

$$\chi^2 = \Sigma \frac{(O-E)^2}{E}$$

$$= \frac{(83-126)^2}{126} + \frac{(169-126)^2}{126}$$

$$= 29.35 \qquad [\chi^2_{.05(1)} = 3.84]$$

Reject H_0 and conclude that the children did not chose dolls at random (at least with respect to color).

It is interesting to note that this particular study played an important role in Brown v. Board of Education (1954). In that case the U.S. Supreme Court ruled that the principle of "separate but equal", which had been the rule supporting segregation in the public schools, was no longer acceptable. Studies such as those of the Clarks had illustrated the negative effects of segregation on self esteem and other variables.

6.7 Combining the two racial choice experiments:

		Black	White	Total
Study	1939	83	169	252
		(106.42)	(145.58)	
	1970	61	28	89
		(37.58)	(51.42)	
		144	197	$341 = N$

$$\chi^2 = \Sigma \frac{(O-E)^2}{E}$$

$$= \frac{(83-106.42)^2}{106.42} + \frac{(169-145.58)^2}{145.58} + \frac{(61-37.58)^2}{37.58} + \frac{(28-51.42)^2}{51.42}$$

$$= 5.154 + 3.768 + 14.595 + 10.667$$

$$= 34.184 \qquad [\chi^2_{.05(1)} = 3.84]$$

Or, using the special formula for 2 * 2 tables:

$$\chi^2 = \frac{N(AD - BC)^2}{(A+B)(C+D)(A+C)(B+D)}$$

$$= \frac{341(83*28 - 169*61)^2}{(252)(89)(144)(197)} = 34.173$$

Reject the H_0 and conclude that the distribution of choices between Black and White dolls was different in the two studies. Choice is *not* independent of Study. We are no longer asking whether one color of doll is preferred over the other color, but whether the *pattern* of preference is constant across studies. In analysis of variance terms we are dealing with an interaction.

> This is the more common use of chi-square—to investigate contingency tables. The important thing to remember about a contingency table is that we are asking whether the pattern of choices across one row (or column) is similar to the pattern of choices across others rows (or columns). We want to know if choices differ as a function of the second variable.

6.9 **a.** Take a group of subjects at random and sort them by gender and life style (categorized three ways).

b. Deliberately take an equal number of males and females and ask them to specify a preference among 3 types of life style.

c. Deliberately take 10 males and 10 females and have them divide themselves into two teams of 10 players each.

> Hint: You can say that you have fixed marginals whenever you know what the marginal (row or column) totals will be even before you run the experiment.

6.11 Cutting the cell sizes in half:

   a. $\chi^2 = 5.153$ (depending on how (or whether) you round fractional values.)

   b. This demonstrates that the obtained value of χ^2 is cut exactly in half, while the critical value remains the same. Thus the sample size plays a very important role, with larger samples being more likely to produce significant results—as is also true of other tests.

> You will find in all of the tests that we will cover, that the likelihood of obtaining a significant difference will increase with the sample size. It just does it more neatly in chi-square. We will have more to say about this when we discuss power in Chapter 8.

6.13 Formula for 2 * 2 tables applied to data in Exercise 6.11:

$$\chi^2 = \frac{N(AD - BC)^2}{(A+B)(C+D)(A+C)(B+D)}$$

$$= \frac{302[(22)(74) - (187)(19)]^2}{(209)(93)(41)(261)} = 5.38$$

6.15 The relationship of assistance-seeking behavior to number of bystanders:

		Sought Assistance		
		Yes	No	Total
	0	11	2	13
		(7.75)	(5.25)	
Number of	1	16	10	26
Bystanders		(15.5)	(10.5)	
	4	4	9	13
		(7.75)	(5.25)	
		31	21	52 = N

$$\chi^2 = \Sigma \frac{(O-E)^2}{E}$$

$$= \frac{(11-7.75)^2}{7.75} + \frac{(2-5.25)^2}{5.25} + \ldots + \frac{(9-5.25)^2}{5.25}$$

$$= 7.908 \qquad [\chi^2_{.05(2)} = 5.99]$$

Reject H_0. The number of bystanders influences whether or not subjects seek help.

6.17 **a.** Weight preference in adolescent girls:

	Reducers	Maintainers	Gainers	Total
White	352	152	31	535
	(336.7)	(151.9)	(46.4)	
Black	47	28	24	99
	(62.3)	(28.1)	(8.6)	
	399	180	55	634 = N

$$\chi^2 = \Sigma \frac{(O-E)^2}{E}$$

$$= \frac{(352 - 336.7)^2}{336.7} + \frac{(152 - 151.9)^2}{151.9} + \ldots + \frac{(24 - 8.6)^2}{8.6}$$

$$= 37.141 \qquad [\chi^2_{.05(2)} = 5.99]$$

Adolescents girls' preferred weight varies with race.

b. The number of girls desiring to lose weight was far in excess of the number of girls who were overweight.

> This is an interesting finding from several points of view, but it is particularly important to us here because it suggests that if we were to study weight or body image, we need to be careful to take ethnic differences into account. We can't just assume that all subjects we get will have about the same opinion. It is usually easy to take a second (or third) variable into account—we just have to know when it is important to do so, and when it isn't.

6.19 Analyzing Exercise 6.12 (Regular or Remedial English and frequency of ADD diagnosis) using the likelihood-ratio approach:

	Never	2nd	4th	2 & 4	5th	2 & 5	4 & 5	2,4,&5	Total
Rem.	22	2	1	3	2	4	3	4	41
Reg.	187	17	11	9	16	7	8	6	261
	209	19	12	12	18	11	11	10	302

$$\chi^2 = 2\left(\Sigma O_{ij} \ln\left[\frac{O_{ij}}{E_{ij}}\right]\right)$$

$$= 2[22 \times \ln(22/28.374) + 2 \times \ln(2/2.579) + \ldots + 6 \times \ln(6/8.642)]$$

$$= 2[22(-.25443) + 2(-0.25444) + \cdots + 6(-0.36492)]$$

$$= 12.753 \text{ on } 7 \text{ } df$$

Do not reject H_0.

6.21 Monday Night Football opinions, before and after watching:

As the data are originally presented, chi-square would not be appropriate because the observations are not independent. The same subjects contribute twice to the data matrix.

6.23 **b.** Row percents take entries as a percentage of row totals, while column percents take entries as percentage of column totals.

c. These are the probabilities (to 4 decimal places) of a $\chi^2 \geq \chi^2_{obt}$.

d. The correlation between the two variables is approximately .25.

6.25 For data in Exercise 6.24a:
a. $\phi_C = \sqrt{26.90/22071} = .0349$

b. Odds Fatal | Placebo = 18/11034 = .00163.
Odds Fatal | Aspirin = 5/11037 = .000453.
Odds Ratio = .00163/.000453 = 3.598
You are 3.6 times more likely to die from a myocardial infarction if you do not take aspirin.

> I can say much the same thing about odds ratios that I said about stem-and-leaf displays. They are intended to make things more meaningful to you and to others. There are different ways of forming many odds ratios. You just have to find one that makes intuitive sense to you.

6.27 For Table 6.4 the odds ratios for smoking as a function of gender = (150/500)/(100/500) = 1.5. Men are 1.5 times more likely to smoke than women.

For Table 6.5 the odds of being the primary shopper as a function of gender = (15/19)/(4/19) = 3.75. Women are 3.75 more likely to be the primary shopper. This gender difference is much more extreme than it was for smoking.

6.29 Dabbs and Morris (1990) study of testosterone.

		Testosterone		
		High	Normal	Total
Delinquency	No	345 (395.723)	3614 (3563.277)	3959
	Yes	101 (50.277)	402 (452.723)	503
		446	4016	4462 = N

$$\chi^2 = \Sigma \frac{(O-E)^2}{E}$$

$$= \frac{(345-395.723)^2}{395.723} + \frac{(3614-3563.277)^2}{3563.277} + \frac{(101-50.277)^2}{50.277} + \frac{(402-452.723)^2}{452.723}$$

$$= 64.08 \qquad [\chi^2_{.05(1)} = 3.84] \text{ Reject } H_0.$$

6.31 Childhood delinquency in the Dabbs and Morris (1990) study.

a.

		Testosterone		
		High	Normal	Total
Delinquency	No	366 (391.824)	3554 (3528.176)	3920
	Yes	80 (54.176)	462 (487.824)	542
		446	4016	4462 = N

$$\chi^2 = \Sigma \frac{(O-E)^2}{E}$$

$$= \frac{(366-391.824)^2}{391.824} + \frac{(3554-3528.176)^2}{3528.176} + \frac{(80-54.176)^2}{54.176} + \frac{(462-487.824)^2}{487.824}$$

$$= 15.57 \qquad [\chi^2_{.05(1)} = 3.84] \text{ Reject } H_0.$$

b. There is a significant relationship between high levels of testosterone in adult men and a history of delinquent behavior during childhood.

c. This result shows that we can tie the two variables (delinquency and testosterone) together historically.

6.33 Gender vs. College in Mireault's (1990) data.

b.

	College					
	1	2	3	4	5	Total
Male	68	0	18	35	4	125
Female	95	21	6	37	16	175
	163	21	24	72	20	$300 = N$

$$\chi^2 = 31.263 \qquad (p = .000)$$

c. The distribution of students across the different colleges in the University varies as a function of gender.

6.35 a. I would agree with the researcher. The probability of a Type I error is held at α, regardless of the sample size.

b. The reviewer is forgetting that the greater variability in the means of small samples is compensated for in the sampling distribution of the test statistic.

c. I would calculate the *number* of people in each category who sided with, *and against*, the researcher.

d. The level of accuracy varies by group ($\chi^2_{.05}(3) = 11.95$) Actually the students numerically outperform the other groups.

> I put this exercise in to make the point that reducing your sample size does not affect the probability of a Type I error. Assuming that you have run the study properly, that probability remains at α regardless of the sample size. BUT, small sample sizes do have a tremendous effect on power, and thus the probability of a Type II error. (These are actual data, by the way. Many people who should know better make this mistake.)

6.37-38 I am trying to get students to think about the issues of measurement and about what we can, and cannot, tell from data. For Exercise 6.37, I would like you to consider plotting the data by assigning values (such as 1 = Never, 2 = Fairly Often, etc.) to the observations. In Exercise 6.38, if scale points mean different things to different sexes, it is possible that the relationship could be distorted by the closed-end nature of the scales.

Chapter 7 - Hypothesis Tests Applied to Means

7.1 Distribution of 100 random numbers:

Number	Frequency
0	11
1	17
2	7
3	9
4	8
5	13
6	7
7	10
8	11
9	7

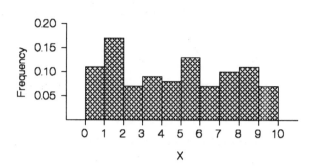

7.3 Does the Central Limit Theorem work?

Population Parameters	Predictions from Central Limit Theorem	Empirical Sampling Distribution
$\mu = 4.18$	$\overline{X} = \mu = 4.18$	$\overline{X} = 4.15$
$\sigma^2 = 8.533$	$s^2 = \dfrac{\sigma^2}{N} = \dfrac{8.533}{5} = 1.707$	$s^2 = 2.022$

The mean of the sampling distribution is very close to that predicted by the Central Limit Theorem. The variance of the sampling distribution is a little high, but it is still approximately correct.

> Remember, the sampling distribution of the mean tells us what the distribution of means will look like. The distribution will have a mean equal to the population mean, but its standard deviation will equal the population's standard deviation divided by the square root of N.

33

7.5 Arizona math SAT:

$$z = \frac{\overline{X} - \mu}{\sigma_{\overline{X}}}$$

$$= \frac{524 - 500}{\frac{100}{\sqrt{2345}}} = 11.62 \quad p = .0000 \quad \text{We would reject } H_0.$$

7.7 Women's salaries: $\overline{X} = 25.1$, $s^2 = 38.77$

$$t = \frac{\overline{X} - \mu}{\sqrt{\frac{s^2}{N}}} = \frac{25.1 - 28}{\sqrt{\frac{38.77}{10}}} = -1.47$$

$$t_{.025(9)} = \pm 2.26 > 1.47 \quad \text{Do not reject } H_0.$$

7.9 For the North Dakota verbal SAT data in Exercise 7.4:

$$CI_{.95} = \overline{X} + z_{.025}\sigma_{\overline{X}}$$

$$= 525 \pm (1.96)(100/\sqrt{238}) = 525 \pm 12.7$$

$$512.3 <= \mu <= 537.7$$

> Remember, we do not conclude that the population mean lies between 512.3 and 537.7 with $p = .95$, because the population mean does not have a probability associated with it. Instead, we conclude that the probability is .95 that an interval *formed in the way we formed this one* will enclose the population mean. If you think that this is splitting hairs, I would have to agree with you.

7.11 Testing the experimental hypothesis that children tend to give socially-approved responses:

a. I would compare the mean of this group to the mean of a population of children tested under normal conditions.

b. The null hypothesis would be that these children come from a population with a mean of 3.87 (the mean of children in general). The research hypothesis would be that these children give socially-approved responses at a different rate from normal children because of the stress they are under.

c.

$$t = \frac{\overline{X} - \mu}{s_{\overline{X}}} = \frac{\overline{X} - \mu}{\frac{s}{\sqrt{N}}}$$

$$= \frac{4.39 - 3.87}{\frac{2.61}{\sqrt{36}}} = \frac{0.52}{0.435} = 1.20$$

With 35 *df* the critical value of *t* at $\alpha = .05$, two-tailed, is 2.03. We retain H_0 and conclude that we have no reason to think that these stressed children give socially-approved answers at a higher than normal rate.

7.13 Self-care skills taught through imitation and physical guidance:

Subject	Diff.
1	4
2	-2
3	4
4	3
5	1
6	3
7	5
8	-4
9	-2
10	7
11	5
12	-1
13	0
14	5
15	0

$$\overline{D} = \frac{\Sigma D}{N} = \frac{28}{15} = 1.87$$

$$s = \sqrt{\frac{200 - \frac{28^2}{15}}{14}} = 3.25$$

$$t = \frac{\overline{D} - 0}{\frac{s_D}{\sqrt{N}}} = \frac{1.87}{\frac{3.25}{\sqrt{15}}} = 2.226 \quad [t_{.025(14)} = \pm 2.145]$$

Reject H_0 and conclude that physical guidance has reduced the assistance required.

7.15 The study would be improved if half the subjects had the two conditions in reversed order.

> The point is to counter-balance the order of treatments so as to at least be able to see if order is important. We will not eliminate any effects of order—they will still be there—but if we know about them we can take them into account.

7.17 Effectiveness of advertising campaign to reduce smoking:

Subject	Diff.
1	2
2	-4
3	3
4	3
5	5
6	0
7	-1
8	-3
9	3
10	-1
11	2
12	-4
13	-1
14	3
15	-2

$$\overline{D} = \frac{\Sigma D}{N} = \frac{5}{15} = 0.33$$

$$s_D = \sqrt{\frac{117 - \frac{25^2}{15}}{14}} = 2.87$$

$$t = \frac{\overline{D} - 0}{\frac{s_D}{\sqrt{N}}} = \frac{0.33}{\frac{2.87}{\sqrt{15}}} = 0.45$$

$$[t_{.025^{(14)}} = \pm 2.145; \text{ do not reject } H_0]$$

7.19 The data in Exercise 7.17 show that the program was not successful and had little effect on smokers. The data in Exercise 7.18 show larger effects. However, the program seems to have been successful for some subjects and to have led other subjects to smoke even more. These two results have cancelled each other out and led to a nonsignificant t. The next step would be to examine the two groups differentiated in Exercise 7.18 to see how they differed. Did the program decrease smoking in women and increase it in men, were there differences between short-term and long-term smokers, and so on.

7.21 Are English grades higher than overall GPA in the Data Set?

Subject	ENGG	GPA	Diff.
1	3	2.60	0.40
2	3	2.75	0.25
3	4	4.00	0.00
4	2	2.25	-0.25
5	3	3.00	0.00
6	2	1.67	0.33
7	2	2.25	-0.25
8	4	3.40	0.60
9	1	1.33	-0.33
10	4	3.50	0.50
11	4	3.75	0.25
12	3	2.67	0.33
13	3	2.75	0.25
14	2	2.00	0.00
15	3	2.75	0.25

$$\overline{D} = \frac{2.28}{20} = 0.114$$

$$s_D = \sqrt{\frac{2.7992 - \frac{2.28^2}{20}}{19}} = 0.366$$

$$t = \frac{\overline{D} - 0}{\frac{s_D}{\sqrt{N}}} = \frac{0.114}{\frac{0.366}{\sqrt{20}}} = 1.395$$

$$[t_{.025^{(19)}} = \pm 2.09] \text{ Do not reject } H_0.$$

16	2	2.50	-0.50
17	4	3.55	0.45
18	3	2.75	0.25
19	4	3.50	0.50
20	2	2.75	-0.75

> Elsewhere we worry about the fact that the variance of English grades will be more that the variance of the overall GPA because of the fact that a GPA is a mean across 4 or 5 individual grades. Notice that this is not a problem here because we are using the difference scores, and not the ENGG and GPA themselves.

7.23 Imitation versus physical guidance in learning self-help skills; different subjects in each group:

$$\overline{X}_1 = \frac{147}{15} = 9.8 \qquad\qquad \overline{X}_2 = \frac{103}{15} = 6.87$$

$$s_1^2 = \frac{1921 - \frac{(147)^2}{15}}{14} \qquad\qquad s_2^2 = \frac{1093 - \frac{(103)^2}{15}}{14}$$

$$= 34.31 \qquad\qquad = 27.55$$

$$t = \frac{\overline{X}_1 - \overline{X}_2}{\sqrt{\dfrac{s_1^2}{N_1} - \dfrac{s_2^2}{N_2}}}$$

$$= \frac{9.8 - 6.87}{\dfrac{34.31}{15} - \dfrac{27.55}{15}}$$

$$= 1.44 \quad [t_{.025(28)} = +2.048] \quad \text{Do not reject } H_0.$$

> One of the biggest problems students have is the question of whether or not to treat a set of data as coming from matched or independent samples. One of the problems that instructors have is that it seems so obvious that they can't figure out what needs clarifying.
>
> This problem contained a giveaway because the data were presented as coming from different subjects under the two conditions. It is almost always true that when we have different subjects in different groups, then we have an independent sample test. (There are exceptions, such as when we interview spouses, and treat the spousal pair as the unit of analysis.)
>
> Perhaps the easiest thing to say is that whenever we can think of "pairs" of scores, then we are talking about matched sample tests. Or, if we can easily imagine there being unequal numbers of observations in the two (or more) groups, then we have independent samples. I would suggest that you try to come up with reasonable examples of each kind of design, and then check with your instructor to see if you're right.

7.25 By measuring the same subject under both conditions in Exercise 7.13 we were able to eliminate subject-to-subject variability.

7.27 We use random assignment to try to protect against the possibility that people who are good at generating solutions would be disproportionately assigned to one of the groups, as could happen if we allowed family members or friends living in the same neighborhood to choose to be in the same group.

> Remember the difference between random assignment and random selection. In many ways random assignment is the more important of the two. See the discussion on pages 2 and 3 of the text.

7.29 Confidence limits for the experimenter bias effect data in Exercise 7.28:

$$CI_{.95} = (\overline{X}_1 - \overline{X}_2) \pm t_{.025}\sqrt{\frac{s_p^2}{N_1} + \frac{s_p^2}{N_2}}$$

$$= (18.778 - 17.625) \pm (2.131)\sqrt{\frac{16.362}{9} + \frac{16.362}{8}} = 1.153 \pm 4.189$$

$$-3.036 \leq (\mu_1 - \mu_2 \leq 5.342$$

7.31 GPAs compared for ADDSC ≤ 65 versus ADDSC ≥ 66:

ADDSC ≤ 65 ADDSC ≥ 66

$$\overline{X} = \frac{194.30}{75} = 2.59 \qquad \frac{21.85}{13} = 1.68 \qquad \text{[Calculated from Data Set]}$$

$N = $ 75   13

$s^2 = $ 0.658   0.56

$$s_p^2 = \frac{(N_1 - 1)s_1^2 + (N_2 - 1)s_2^2}{N_1 + N_2 - 2}$$

$$= \frac{74(.658) + 12(.56)}{86} = .644$$

$$t = \frac{\overline{X}_1 - \overline{X}_2}{\sqrt{\dfrac{s_p^2}{N_1} + \dfrac{s_p^2}{N_2}}} = \frac{2.59 - 1.68}{\sqrt{\dfrac{.6443}{75} + \dfrac{.6443}{13}}} = 3.77 \qquad t_{.025(86)} = \pm 1.984$$

reject H_0

> The fact that this difference in grade point average between those who had high ADDSC scores and those who had lower ones is significant, tells us that ADDSC is a significant (and important) predictor of performance much later in school.

7.33 Innate ability versus time-filling tasks; dependent variable = number of problems solved:

$$\overline{X}_1 = \frac{27}{5} = 5.4 \qquad N_1 = 5 \qquad s_1^2 = \frac{163 - \dfrac{27^2}{5}}{4} = 4.3$$

$$\overline{X}_2 = \frac{42}{5} = 8.4 \qquad N_2 = 5 \qquad s_2^2 = \frac{368 - \dfrac{42^2}{5}}{4} = 3.8$$

$$t = \frac{\overline{X}_1 - \overline{X}_2}{\sqrt{\dfrac{s_1^2}{N_1} + \dfrac{s_2^2}{N_2}}} = \frac{5.4 - 8.4}{\sqrt{\dfrac{4.3}{5} + \dfrac{3.8}{5}}} = -2.36 \qquad [t_{.025(8)} = \pm 2.306]$$

Reject H_0.

7.35 Perfectly legitimate and reasonable transformations of data can produce different results. It is important to consider seriously the nature of the dependent variable before beginning an experiment.

> Again, I am beating on the idea that how we measure things is important. It makes a difference whether we measure minutes/problem or problems/minute, and yet neither is obviously a more appropriate measure than the other. (In some parts of the world people speak of miles per gallon, and in other parts they speak of gallons/mile (or its equivalent).)

7.37 Computer exercise. GPA would be expected to have a smaller variance because it is a mean across a number of courses, and the central limit theorem tells us that the variance of means is smaller than the variance of individual observations that make up those means.

7.39 b. The tests are not independent because the data came from the same subjects and because the Global Symptom Index is based on the sum of the subscales.

7.41 Computer exercise.

7.43 This question again gets at the issues of measurement. It points up the question of how we measure a variable, as well as forcing people to think about what the statistical test tells us. I would like students to see that we are asking entirely different questions here and in Chapter 6.

Chapter 8 - Power

8.1 Mean SAT for entering freshmen at small N.E. college:

a.
$$d = \frac{\mu_1 - \mu_0}{\sigma}$$
$$= \frac{520 - 500}{80}$$
$$= .25$$

b. $f(N)$ for 1-sample t-test $= \sqrt{N}$

$$\delta = d\sqrt{N}$$
$$= .25\sqrt{100}$$
$$= 2.5$$

c. Power $= .71$

8.3 Changing power in Exercise 8.1:

a. For power $= .70$, $\delta = 2.475$

$$\delta = d\sqrt{N}$$
$$2.475 = .25\sqrt{N}$$
$$N = 98.01 = 99 \text{ (Round up, since students generally come in whole lots.)}$$

b. For power $= .80$, $\delta = 2.8$

$$\delta = d\sqrt{N}$$
$$2.8 = .25\sqrt{N}$$
$$N = 125.44 = 126 \text{ (Round up)}$$

c. For power $= .90$, $\delta = 3.25$

$$\delta = d\sqrt{N}$$
$$3.25 = .25\sqrt{N}$$
$$N = 169$$

8.5 Sampling distributions of the mean for the situation in Exercise 8.4:

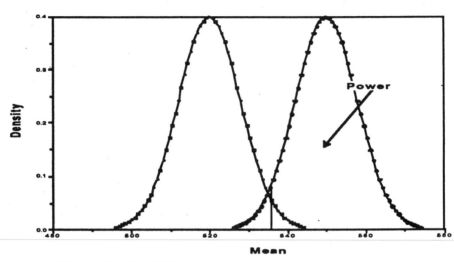

Power if Mean SAT = 550

8.7 Avoidance behavior in rabbits using 1-sample t test:

a.
$$d = \frac{\mu_1 - \mu_0}{\delta} = \frac{5.8 - 4.8}{2} = \frac{1}{2} = .5$$

For power = .50, $\delta = 1.95$

$$\delta = d\sqrt{N}$$
$$1.95 = .5\sqrt{N}$$
$$N = 15.21 \approx 16$$

b. For power = .80, $\delta = 2.8$

$$\delta = \mathbf{d}\sqrt{N}$$
$$2.8 = .5\sqrt{N}$$
$$N = 31.36 \approx 32$$

8.9 Avoidance behavior in rabbits with unequal Ns:

$$\mathbf{d} = .5$$

$$N = \overline{N}_h = \frac{2N_1N_2}{N_1 + N_2}$$

$$= \frac{2(20)(15)}{20 + 15} = 17.14$$

$$\delta = \mathbf{d}\sqrt{\frac{N}{2}} = .5\sqrt{\frac{17.14}{2}} = 1.46$$

power = .31

8.11 t test on data for Exercise 8.10

$$t = \frac{\overline{X}_1 - \overline{X}_2}{\sqrt{\dfrac{s_p^2}{n_1} + \dfrac{s_p^2}{n_2}}}$$

$$= \frac{25 - 30}{\sqrt{\dfrac{64}{20} + \dfrac{64}{20}}}$$

$$= -1.98 \qquad\qquad [t_{.025(38)} = \pm 2.025] \quad \text{Do not reject } H_0.$$

c. t is numerically equal to δ although t is calculated from statistics and δ is calculated from parameters. In other words, δ = the t that you would get if the data exactly match what you think are the values of the parameters.

> This relationship between t and δ is important. It follows directly from the formulae, but most people wouldn't notice that because of the way we separate the sample size from the rest of the calculation of δ,

8.13 Diagram to defend answer to Exercise 8.12:

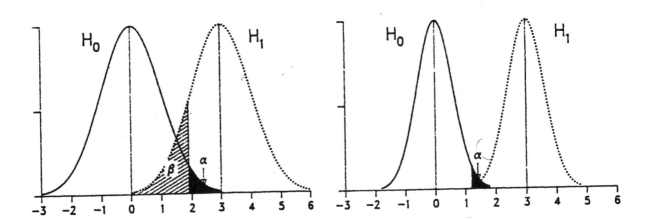

With larger sample sizes the sampling distribution of the mean has a smaller standard error, which means that there is less overlap of the distributions. This results in greater power, and therefore the larger N's significant result was less impressive.

8.15 Social awareness of ex-delinquents--which subject pool would be better to use?

$$\overline{X}_{normal} = 38 \qquad N = 50$$
$$\overline{X}_{H.S. Grads.} = 35 \qquad N = 100$$
$$\overline{X}_{dropout} = 30 \qquad N = 25$$

$$d = \frac{38 - 35}{\sigma} \qquad\qquad\qquad d = \frac{38 - 30}{\sigma}$$

$$\overline{N}_h = \frac{2(50)(100)}{150} = 66.67 \qquad\qquad \overline{N}_h = \frac{2(50)(25)}{75} = 33.33$$

$$\delta = \frac{3}{\sigma}\sqrt{\frac{66.67}{2}} = \frac{17.32}{\sigma} \qquad\qquad \delta = \frac{3}{\sigma}\sqrt{\frac{33.33}{2}} = \frac{32.66}{\sigma}$$

Assuming equal standard deviations, the H.S. dropout group of 25 would result in a higher value of δ and therefore higher power. (You can let σ be any value you choose, as long as it is the same for both calculations. Then calculate δ for each situation.)

> This exercise illustrates the relationship between sample size, effect size, and power.

8.17 Total sample sizes required for power = .60, α = .05, two-tailed (δ = 2.2):

Effect Size	d	One-sample t	Two-sample t Per Group	Two-sample t Overall
Small	0.2	120	242	484
Medium	0.5	20	39	78
Large	0.8	8	16	32

8.19 When can power = β?

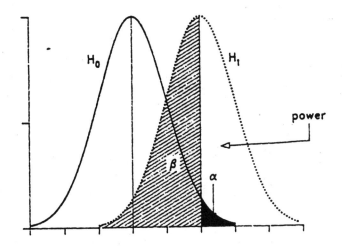

The mean under H_1 should fall at the critical value under H_0. The question implies a one-tailed test. Thus the mean is 1.645 standard errors above μ_0, which is 100.

$$\mu = 100 + 1.645\sigma_x$$

$$= 100 + 1.645(15/\sqrt{25}$$

$$= 104.935$$

When μ = 104.935, power would equal β.

I cannot stress enough the importance of drawing diagrams. That's the way I solve these problems, and I've been at it for a long time.

45

8.21 **a.** For power = .80, we need to have $\delta = 2.80$ in all cases.

For $\delta = 2.80$, and $N = 50$,

$$\delta = d\sqrt{N/2}$$

$$2.80 = d\sqrt{50/2}$$

$$d = 2.80/\sqrt{25} = 0.56$$

d must equal 0.56 for power to equal .80

b.

$$d = \frac{\mu_1 - \mu_2}{\sigma} = 0.5$$

$$0.56 = (\mu_1 = \mu_2)/10$$

$$(\mu_1 - \mu_2) = 5.6$$

You would have to add 5.6 points to one of the variables to produce a test with power = .80.

8.23 I don't see that Prentice and Miller (1992) are really talking about experiments with small power. They are talking about relatively small experimental manipulations, but those manipulations are sufficient to generate enough of a group difference for the effect to be apparent.

Here I am trying to get students to think about what we mean by power and what we mean by small effects. I would also like you to come to realize that we don't have to find a huge difference between two means for the result to be meaningful.

Chapter 9 - Correlation and Regression

9.1 Scatter diagram of percentage of LBW infants (Y) and high-risk fertility rate (X_1) in Vermont Health Planning Districts.

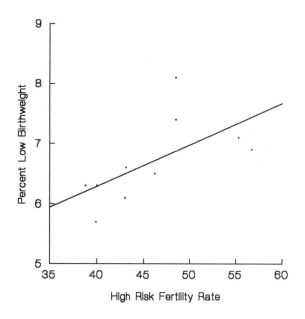

> In plotting this figure, we put High Risk Fertility Rate on the abscissa (X axis) because that serves as the basis for the prediction. The Percent Low Birthweight is on the ordinate (Y axis) because that is the dependent variable. It wouldn't really make sense to try to predict how many women are in the high risk group by looking at birthweight data, because the causal connection (if any) would certainly be the other way around.

9.3 Correlation between percentage of LBW infants (Y) and percentage of births to unmarried mothers (X_2) in Vermont Health Planning Districts.

$$N = 10 \qquad \Sigma X_2 Y = 689.62$$

$$\Sigma X_2 = 102.5 \qquad \Sigma X_2^2 = 1066.35$$

$$\Sigma Y = 67 \qquad \Sigma Y^2 = 453.28$$

$$s_Y = \sqrt{\frac{\Sigma Y^2 - \frac{(\Sigma Y)^2}{N}}{N-1}} = \sqrt{\frac{453.28 - \frac{67^2}{10}}{9}} = 0.698$$

$$s_{X_2} = \sqrt{\frac{\Sigma X_2^2 - \frac{(\Sigma X_2)^2}{N}}{N-1}} = \sqrt{\frac{1066.35 - \frac{102.5^2}{10}}{9}} = 1.322$$

$$\text{cov}_{X_2 Y} = \frac{\Sigma X_2 Y - \frac{\Sigma X_2 \Sigma Y}{N}}{N-1} = \frac{689.62 - \frac{(102.5)(67)}{10}}{9} = 0.3189$$

$$r = \frac{\text{cov}_{X_2 Y}}{s_{X_2} s_Y} = \frac{0.3189}{(1.322(0.698))} = .35$$

9.5   Three sets of data:

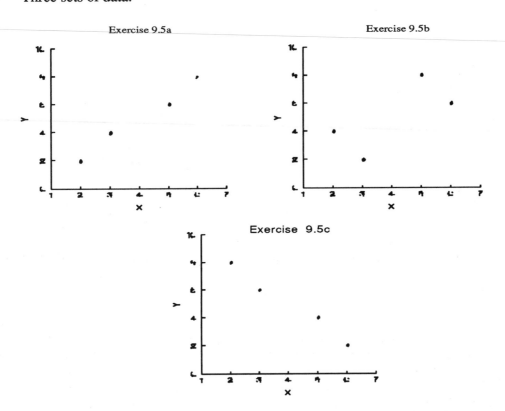

a. Covariances using definitional formula:

$$cov_{XY} = \frac{\Sigma(X - \overline{X})(Y - \overline{Y})}{N - 1}$$

	Set 1				Set 2				Set 3		
	X		Y		X		Y		X		Y
	2	-2	2	-3	2	-2	4	-1	2	-2	8	3
	3	-1	4	-1	3	-1	2	-3	3	-1	6	1
	5	1	6	1	5	1	8	3	5	1	4	-1
	6	2	8	3	6	2	6	1	6	2	2	-3
$\Sigma()$:	16		20		16		20		16		20	
Mean:	4		5		4		5		4		5	

$\Sigma(X - \overline{X})(Y - \overline{Y})$:

14   10   -14

ΣX^2:	74	120	74	120	74	120
ΣXY:	94		90		66	

cov_{XY}:

$$= \frac{14}{3} = 4.67 \qquad = \frac{10}{3} = 3.33 \qquad = \frac{-14}{3} = -4.67$$

b. Covariances using computational formula:

$$cov_{XY} = \frac{\Sigma XY - \dfrac{\Sigma X \Sigma Y}{N}}{N - 1}$$

$$cov_{XY} = \frac{94 - \dfrac{16(20)}{4}}{3} \qquad = \frac{90 - \dfrac{16(20)}{4}}{3} \qquad = \frac{66 - \dfrac{16(20)}{4}}{3}$$

$$= 4.67 \qquad\qquad = 3.33 \qquad\qquad = -4.67$$

9.7 Yes. The coefficient (*r*) would still tell you how well a straight line fits, even if you think that a curved line would fit better. Often the fit of a straight line is sufficiently good for our purposes.

> Many of the relationships that we look at are really curvilinear in some way, because curves tend to flatten out at the extremes. But in practice we do very well by just solving for linear relationships and ignoring the slightly poorer fit at the extremes. But if curvilinearity is theoretically important, go ahead and solve for it.

9.9 Regression equation predicting Y (percentage of births of infants under 2500 grams) from X_1 (high risk fertility rate) from Exercise 9.1:

$$b = \frac{\text{cov}_{XY}}{s_X^2}$$

$$= \frac{2.727}{39.552} = .0689$$

$$\text{cov}_{XY} = \frac{\Sigma XY - \dfrac{\Sigma X \Sigma Y}{N}}{N} - 1$$

$$a = \frac{\Sigma Y - b\Sigma X}{N}$$

$$= \frac{3106.54 - \dfrac{67(460)}{10}}{9} = 2.727$$

$$= \frac{67 - .0689(460)}{10}$$

$$s_X^2 = 39.552$$

$$s_X = 6.29$$

$$= 3.53$$

$$\hat{Y} = bX + a = 0.0689X + 3.53$$

9.11

$$CI(b^*) = b \pm t_{\alpha/2}(s_{Y.X}) / s_X\sqrt{(N-1)}$$

$$= 0.0689 \pm 2.306(0.580 / (6.289\sqrt{9}))$$

$$= 0.0689 \pm 0.0709$$

$$-0.0020 \le b \le 0.1398$$

> Notice that these limits include 0.00. This is itself a test on the null hypothesis that the true value of b in the population is 0, and is perfectly consistent with the standard test of b *.

9.13 We would be extrapolating way beyond the range of the data on which the equation is based.

> Remember that confidence limits on a regression line are elliptical, departing further and further from the line as X becomes more extreme. Also keep in mind that any curvilinearity that is present will show up in the extremes.

9.15 Number of symptoms predicted for a mean stress score using the data in Table 9.2 (page 238):

Regression equation (page 243): $\hat{Y} = 0.7831X + 73.891$

If Stress score (X) = 21.467: $\hat{Y} = 0.7831(21.467) + 73.891$

Predicted Number of symptoms: $\hat{Y} = 90.701$, which is equal to $\overline{Y}$.

> The regression line will always go through the point $\overline{X}, \overline{Y}$, and thus our prediction of Y will always be $\overline{Y}$ when $X = \overline{X}$.

9.17 The regression equation for faculty shows that the best estimate of starting salary for faculty is $15,000 (the intercept in the equation). For every additional year of service salary increases on average by $900 (the slope). For administrative staff the best estimate of starting salary is $10,000 (the intercept), but every year of additional service increases the salary by an average of $1500 (the slope). They will be equal at 8 1/3 years of service.

9.19 Power for study of relationship of number of days skiing and mental health rating:

$$\delta = \rho_1 \sqrt{N - 1}$$
$$= .40 \sqrt{30 - 1} = 2.154$$

Power = 0.58

9.21 a. Included in Minitab output, but not SPSS:

Complete regression equation.
Intercept, its standard deviation, and a *t*-test on it.
Total *df* and SS in Analysis of Variance.
Observations with large standardized residuals or whose X values give them large influence.

b. Included in SPSS output, but not in Minitab:

Intercorrelation matrix.
Unsquared correlation coefficient.

9.23 $r_1 = .88$ $r'_1 = 1.376$

$r_2 = .72$ $r'_2 = .908$

$$z = \frac{r_1' - r_2'}{\sqrt{\dfrac{1}{N_1 - 3} + \dfrac{1}{N_2 - 3}}} = \frac{1.376 - .908}{\sqrt{\dfrac{1}{49} + \dfrac{1}{71}}}$$
$$= 2.52$$

The difference is significant.

> But notice that even for the group who did not read the passage there was a significant correlation between how they did here and how they did on the SATs. ($t = 8.80$ on 72 *df*). This suggests that both this task and the SATs are measuring some of the same stuff—which may simply be the ability to take multiple choice tests.

9.27 a. The correlations range between .40 and .80.

b. The subscales are not measuring independent aspects of psychological well-being.

9.29 When you break the data down by both the gender of the parent and the child, the sample sizes become too small for meaningful analyses.

9.31 Computer problem

9.33 Relationship between height and weight for females:

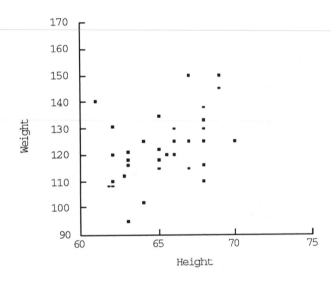

Scatterplot for Females

The regression solution that follows was produced by Systat and gives all relevant results.

```
DEP VAR:   WEIGHT        N:      35  MULTIPLE R: 0.494  SQUARED MULTIPLE R: 0.244
ADJUSTED SQUARED MULTIPLE R: 0.221     STANDARD ERROR OF ESTIMATE:      11.79969
```

VARIABLE	COEFFICIENT	STD ERROR	STD COEF	TOLERANCE	T	P(2 TAIL)
CONSTANT	-44.85892	51.68351	0.00000	.	-0.86795	0.39169
HEIGHT	2.57888	0.78968	0.49421	1.00000	3.26574	0.00255

```
                         ANALYSIS OF VARIANCE

SOURCE          SUM-OF-SQUARES    DF   MEAN-SQUARE     F-RATIO        P

REGRESSION        1484.92057      1    1484.92057     10.66503    0.00255
RESIDUAL          4594.67943     33     139.23271
```

> Remember that the intercept is the predicted weight for a subject who is 0.00 inches tall. Obviously that is a meaningless value. The slope is the change in $\hat{Y}$ for a one unit change in X. Here we are saying that for a 1 unit difference in height we would expect a 2.58 lb. difference in weight. Even though the intercept is meaningless, it still serves to anchor the line. It tells us which of an infinite number of lines with a slope of 2.57888 is the one we want—the one which goes through the point (0, -44.85892).

9.35 The largest residual for males is 51.311 points. This person was 6 feet tall and weighed 215 pounds. His predicted weight was only 163.7 pounds.

9.37 Males are denser. By this I mean that a male weighs more per inch than does a female.

9.39 Air quality measures.

In these data (found as Ex9-39.dat) I wanted students to see that there are many ways of looking at a relationship between variables. Comparing the means would tell us only that one instrument read higher than the other, it wouldn't get at whether they are measuring the same thing. The data are somewhat curvilinear, and we need to take that into account.

> One place you might start in answering this question is to address their original question of whether they should run a t test between the two sets of numbers, and what kind of t test they should run (if any). What question would the t test answer? Then think about what a correlation would tell you, and about the meaning of regression coefficients. And don't stop there.

Chapter 10 - Alternative Correlational Methods

10.1 Performance ratings in the morning related to perceived peak time to day:

a. Plot of data with regression line:

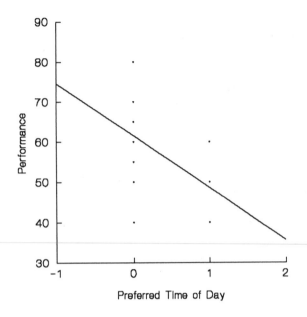

b. $s_X = 0.489$

$s_Y = 11.743$

$\text{cov}_{XY} = -3.105$

$$r_{pb} = \frac{\text{cov}_{XY}}{s_X s_Y} = \frac{-3.105}{(0.489)(11.743)} = -.540$$

$$t = \frac{r\sqrt{(N-2)}}{\sqrt{1-r^2}} = \frac{(-.540)\sqrt{18}}{\sqrt{.708}} = \frac{-2.291}{.842} = -2.723 \quad [p < .01]$$

c. Performance in the morning is significantly related to people's perceptions of their peak periods.

> Notice that the only thing different about this problem and the ones in Chapter 9 is that here *you* know that one of the variables is a dichotomy. I italicized the "you" to emphasis that the statistical procedure has very limited intelligence and *it* doesn't know. The calculations are the same. But the fact that you know about the variables also means that you are responsible for using a procedure correctly.

10.3 It looks as if morning people vary their performance across time, but that evening people are uniformly poor.

10.5 Running a t test on the data in Exercise 10.1:

$$\overline{X}_1 = \frac{800}{13} = 61.538 \quad N_1 = 13 \qquad s_1^2 = \frac{50600 - \frac{800^2}{13}}{12} = 114.103$$

$$\overline{X}_2 = \frac{340}{7} = 48.571 \quad N_2 = 7 \qquad s_2^2 = \frac{17000 - \frac{340^2}{7}}{6} = 80.952$$

$$s_p^2 = \frac{(N_1 - 1)s_1^2 + (N_2 - 1)s_2^2}{N_1 + N_2 - 2}$$

$$= \frac{(13 - 1)(114.103) + (7 - 1)(80.952)}{13 + 7 - 2}$$

$$= 103.053$$

$$t = \frac{\overline{X}_1 - \overline{X}_2}{\sqrt{\frac{s_p^2}{N_1} + \frac{s_p^2}{N_2}}} = \frac{61.538 - 48.571}{\sqrt{\frac{103.053}{13} + \frac{103.053}{7}}} = 2.725 \quad \begin{array}{l} [t_{.025(18)} = \pm 2.101] \\[4pt] \text{Reject } H_0. \end{array}$$

The *t* calculated here (2.725) is equal to the *t* calculated to test the significance of the *r* calculated in Exercise 10.1.

> Keep in mind that this relationship between *t* and r_{pb} must be true, as is the corresponding relationship between phi and χ^2. If two groups differ on some variable, then there is a relationship between group membership and performance.

10.7 Regression equation for relationship between college GPA and completion of Ph.D. program:

$$b = \frac{\text{cov}_{XY}}{s_X^2} = \frac{0.051}{.503^2} = .202$$

$$a = \frac{\Sigma Y - b\Sigma X}{N} = \frac{17 - .202(72.58)}{25} = .093$$

$$\hat{Y} = bX + a = .202X + .093$$

When $X = \overline{X} = 2.9032$, $\hat{Y} = .202(2.9032) + .093 = .680 = \overline{Y}$.

10.9 Establishment of a GPA cutoff of 3.00:

a. Ph.D. (Y): 0 0 0 0 0 0 0 0 1 1 1 1 1 1 1 1 1 1 1 1 1 1 1 1 1
GPA (X): 0 1 0 1 1 0 0 0 1 0 1 1 1 1 0 1 1 1 0 0 0 1 1 1 0

$N = 25$ $\Sigma Y = 17$ $\Sigma Y^2 = 17$ $\Sigma X = 14$ $\Sigma X^2 = 14$ $\Sigma XY = 11$

$$s_X = 0.507$$
$$s_Y = 0.476$$
$$\text{cov}_{XY} = 0.062$$

$$\phi = \frac{0.062}{(0.507)(0.476)} = .256$$

b. $t = \dfrac{r\sqrt{(N-2)}}{\sqrt{1-r^2}} = \dfrac{(.256)\sqrt{23}}{\sqrt{.934}} = \dfrac{1.228}{.967} = 1.27$ [not significant]

10.11 Alcoholism and childhood history of ADD:

a. $N = 32$ $\Sigma X = 10$ $\Sigma X^2 = 10$ $\Sigma Y = 9$ $\Sigma Y^2 = 9$ $\Sigma XY = 7$

$$s_X = 0.471$$
$$s_Y = 0.457$$
$$\text{cov}_{XY} = 0.135$$

$$\phi = \frac{0.135}{(0.471)(0.457)} = .628$$

b. $\chi^2 = N\phi^2 = 32(.628^2) = 12.62$ [$p < .05$]

> Again, I could make the same statement I made after Exercise 10.5. If you keep this in mind, it will simplify your life considerably—well, maybe not your whole life, but part of it.

10.13 Development ordering of language skills using Kendall's τ

a. $\tau = 1 - \dfrac{2(\# \text{ inversions})}{\# \text{ pairs}} = 1 - \dfrac{2(6)}{15(14)/2} = 1 - \dfrac{23}{105} = .886$

b. $z = \dfrac{\tau}{\sqrt{\dfrac{2(2N+5)}{9N(N-1)}}} = \dfrac{.886}{\sqrt{\dfrac{2(30+5)}{9(15)(14)}}} = \dfrac{.886}{\sqrt{.037}} = 4.60 \quad [p < .05]$

10.15 Ranking of videotapes of children's behaviors by clinical graduate students and experienced clinicians using Kendall's τ:

[Before drawing lines to count inversions it is necessary to reorder the data so that one set of rankings are in numerical order.]

$\tau = 1 - \dfrac{2(\# \text{ inversions})}{\# \text{ pairs}} = 1 = \dfrac{2(6)}{10(9)/2} = 1 - \dfrac{12}{45} = .733$

> There are other ways to calculate τ (your friendly computer package doesn't get out its ruler and pencil and start drawing lines), but the method given here is by far the easiest to explain. I have never had much luck explaining other ways of computing the number of inversions, even when I understand them myself.

10.17 Verification of Rosenthal and Rubin's statement

	Improvement	No Improvement	Total
Therapy	66	34	100
No Therapy	34	66	100
Total	100	100	200

a.
$$\chi^2 = \frac{N(AD - BC)^2}{(A+B)(C+D)(A+C)(AB+D)}$$

$$= \frac{200(66*66-34*34)^2}{100*100*100*100} = 20.48$$

b. An $r_2 = .0512$ would correspond to $\chi^2 = 10.24$. You would get such a result if the subjects were split 61/39 in the first condition and 39/61 in the second (rounding to integers.)

> The first part of this problem is straightforward—you just compute the answer using the standard formula for χ^2. The second part is less straightforward. You first have to calculate the appropriate value of χ^2 associated with an $r^2 = .0512$ using the formula on p. 284. Then you need to make up different 2x2 tables until you get one with a χ^2 that is close to what you need. In making up those tables, let the second row be the reverse of the first row. (If the first row is 73 27, then the second is 27 73, and so on.)

10.19 ClinCase against Group in Mireault's data

	ClinCase	
	0	1
Loss	69	66
Married	108	73
Divorced	36	23

a. $\chi^2 = 2.815$ $\qquad$ [$p = .245$]

$\phi_C = .087$

c. This approach would be preferred over the approach used in Chapter 7 if you had reason to believe that differences in depression scores below the clinical cutoff were of no importance and should be ignored.

It is important to note that psychologists often do exactly what I have done in this problem. Sometimes a continuous diagnostic score doesn't tell us very much, but a cutoff point on that score does. It is as if different levels of the predictor aren't associated with differences in behavior *up to some point*, but once you pass that point behavior changes.

10.21 b. If a statistic is not significant, that means that we have no reason to believe that it is reliably different from 0 (or whatever the parameter under H_0). In the case of a correlation, if it is not significant, that means that we have no reason to believe that the is a relationship between the two variables. Therefore it cannot be important.

c. With the exceptions of issues of power, sample size will not make an effect more important than it is. Increasing n will increase our level of significance (the p value), but the magnitude of the effect will be unaffected.

Chapter 11 - Simple Analysis of Variance

11.1 Retrieval of rat pups:

$T_1 = 103$ $\Sigma X = 489$
$T_2 = 133$ $N = 18$
$T_3 = 253$ $n = 6$

$$SS_{total} = \Sigma X^2 - \frac{(\Sigma X)^2}{N}$$

$$= 15777 - \frac{489^2}{18} = 2492.5$$

$$SS_{group} = \frac{\Sigma T_j^2}{n} - \frac{(\Sigma X)^2}{N}$$

$$= \frac{103^2 + 133^2 + 253^2}{6} - \frac{489^2}{18} = 2100$$

$$SS_{error} = SS_{total} - SS_{group}$$

$$= 2492.5 - 2100 = 392.5$$

Source	df	SS	MS	F
Age of Pup	2	2100.0	1050.000	40.127*
Error	15	392.5	26.167	
Total	17	2492.5		

*p < .05 $[F_{.05(2,15)} = 3.68]$

> Notice several things about this problem that will appear in the next several chapters. In the first place, the denominator in calculating SS_{age} is 5, which is the number of scores involved in each group (and hence each treatment total), Note that the sums of squares sum to SS_{total}, which is always the case in a one-way design and in factorial designs with equal sample sizes. Finally, note that MS_{error} forms the denominator for our F.

11.3 Recall in Eysenck (1974) for four Age/Levels of Processing groups:

$T_1 = 65$ $\Sigma X = 448$
$T_2 = 193$ $\Sigma X^2 = 6316$
$T_3 = 70$ $N = 20$
$T_4 = 120$ $n = 10$

a.

$$SS_{total} = \Sigma X^2 - \frac{(\Sigma X)^2}{N}$$

$$= 6316 - \frac{448^2}{40} = 1298.4$$

$$SS_{group} = \frac{\Sigma T_j^2}{n} - \frac{(\Sigma X)^2}{N}$$

$$= \frac{65^2 + ... + 120^2}{10} - \frac{448^2}{40} = 1059.8$$

$$SS_{error} = SS_{total} - SS_{group}$$

$$= 1298.4 - 1059.8 = 238.6$$

Source	df	SS	MS	F
Group	3	1059.80	353.27	53.30*
Error	36	238.60	6.63	
Total	39	1298.4		

$*p < .05 \quad [F_{.05(3,36)} = 2.87]$

b. Groups 1 and 3 combined versus 2 and 4 combined:

$T_1 = 135 \qquad\qquad \Sigma X = 448$
$T_2 = 313 \qquad\qquad \Sigma X^2 = 6316$
$n = 20 \qquad\qquad\;\; N = 44$

$$SS_{total} = \Sigma X^2 - \frac{(\Sigma X)^2}{N}$$

$$= 6316 - \frac{448^2}{40} = 1298.4$$

$$SS_{group} = \frac{\Sigma T_j^2}{n} - \frac{(\Sigma X)^2}{N}$$

$$= \frac{135^2 + 313^2}{20} - \frac{448^2}{40} = 792.1$$

$$SS_{error} = SS_{total} - SS_{group}$$

$$= 1298.4 - 792.1 = 502.3$$

Source	df	SS	MS	F
Group	1	792.1	792.10	59.45*
Error	38	506.3	13.32	
Total	39	1298.4		

$*p < .05 \quad [F_{.05(1,18)} = 4.41]$

c. The results are somewhat difficult to interpret because the error term now includes variance between younger and older subjects. Notice that this is roughly double what it was in part a. In addition, we do not know whether the level of processing effect is true for both age groups, or if it applies primarily to one group.

> This problem is really setting up a similar problem in Chapter 13, where we will break the Group effect down into an Age effect, a Level of processing effect, and their interaction. But I thought that it was important for you to see this first set up as a one-way analysis of variance.

11.5 Rerun of Exercise 11.2 with additional subjects:
The following is abbreviated printout from Systat.

a.

ANALYSIS OF VARIANCE

SOURCE	SUM-OF-SQUARES	DF	MEAN-SQUARE	F-RATIO	P
GROUP	224.5833	1	224.5833	18.8001	0.0003
ERROR	238.9167	20	11.9458		

LEAST SQUARES MEANS.

			LS MEAN	SE	N
GROUP	=	1.0000	18.4167	0.9977	12
GROUP	=	2.0000	12.0000	1.0930	10

b. and c.

INDEPENDENT SAMPLES T-TEST ON   RECALL   GROUPED BY   GROUP

GROUP	N	MEAN	SD
1.0000	12	18.4167	3.2039
2.0000	10	12.0000	3.7417

SEPARATE VARIANCES T =	4.2726 DF =	17.9 PROB =	0.0005
POOLED VARIANCES T =	4.3359 DF =	20 PROB =	0.0003

d. The squared t for the pooled case = $4.3359^2 = 18.80$, which is the F in the analysis of variance.

> What I would like you to see here is the fact that a standard one-way analysis of variance actually pools the sample variances. You could get the same error term if you calculated the variance in each group and then averaged them (using the degrees of freedom within each group as weights, if necessary).

11.7 Magnitude of effect measures for Exercise 11.3a:

$$\eta^2 = \frac{SS_{group}}{SS_{total}} = \frac{1059.8}{1298.4} = .82$$

$$\omega^2 = \frac{SS_{group} - (k-1)MS_{error}}{SS_{total} + MS_{error}} = \frac{1059.8 - (4-1)6.63}{1298.4 + 6.63} = .80$$

1.9 Magnitude of effect for Foa et al (1991) study:

$$\eta^2 = \frac{SS_{group}}{SS_{total}} = \frac{507.840}{2786.907} = .18$$

$$\omega^2 = \frac{SS_{group} - (k-1)MS_{error}}{SS_{total} + MS_{error}} = \frac{507.840 - (4-1)55.587}{2786.907 + 55.587} = .12$$

> You might think that these values look pretty small, accounting for a bit over 10% of the variability in symptom scores. But if you think of all the people you know, you can easily understand that there would be tremendous variability in their reports of symptoms (even without a rape). Rape is extremely traumatic, and many women are   devastated by it. Some would be expected to deal with it effectively while others just can't handle it. There might even be a few women who would not experience many symptoms, though I would doubt that there are many of them. To be able to account for even 10% of the variability in level of symptoms just by the kind of intervention you employ strikes me as being quite an accomplishment.

11.11 The results are basically the same as ours, although we are presented with confidence limits on group means and r^2 (which is really η^2).

11.13 Model for Exercise 11.1:

$$X_{ij} = \mu + \tau_j + e_{ij}$$

where

μ = grand mean
τ_j = the effect of the jth treatment
e_{ij} = the unit of error for the ith subject in treatment$_j$

> The basic idea of a model is that we have to have someplace to start (μ), we have to have the effect of whatever treatment we apply (τ_j), even if that treatment is not particularly effective, and we have to remember that there is error variance associated with each response. The model just puts these ideas together in a logical statement.

11.15 Model for Exercise 11.1:

$$X_{ij} = \mu + \tau_j + e_{ij}$$

where

μ = grand mean
τ_j = the effect of the jth treatment (where a "treatment" is a particular combination of Age and Task.
e_{ij} = the unit of error for the ith subject in treatment j

11.17 Howell & Huessy (1981) study of ADD in elementary school vs. GPA in high school:

Group	Group totals $T_j = n_j \overline{X}_j$	s_j^2	n_j
Never ADD	538.1574	0.9450	201
2nd only	20.9599	1.0195	13
4th only	23.9700	0.5840	12
2nd & 4th	16.2296	0.2982	8
5th only	23.8000	0.7723	14
2nd & 5th	17.1000	1.0646	9
4th & 5th	13.2902	0.0927	7
all 3 yrs	11.3800	0.3462	8
	664.8871		272

$$SS_{treat} = \frac{\Sigma T_j^2}{n_j} - CF = \frac{538.1574^2}{201} + \ldots + \frac{11.3800^2}{8} - \frac{664.8871^2}{272} = 44.5570$$

$$MS_{error} = \frac{\Sigma(n_j - 1)s_j^2}{\Sigma(n_j - 1)} = \frac{200(.9450) + \ldots + 7(.3462)}{200 + 12 + \ldots + 7} = .8761$$

Source	df	SS	MS	F
ADD diagnosis	7	44.5570	6.3653	7.2655*
Error	264	231.2817	0.8761	
Total	271	275.8387		

$p < .05$ $[F_{.05(7,264)} = 2.06]$

11.19 Square Root Transformation of data in Table 11.5:

Original data:	Control	0.1	0.5	1	2
	130	93	510	229	144
	94	444	416	475	111
	225	403	154	348	217
	105	192	636	276	200
	92	67	396	167	84
	190	170	451	151	99
	32	77	376	107	44
	64	353	192	235	84
	69	365	384		284
	93	422			293
Totals	1094	2586	3515	1988	1560
Means	109.4	258.6	390.56	248.5	156
S.D.	58.5	153.32	147.68	118.74	87.65
Var	3421.82	23506.04	21809.78	14098.86	7682.22
n	10	10	9	8	10

Square root transformed data:

	Control	0.1	0.5	1	2	
	11.402	9.644	22.583	15.133	12.000	
	9.695	21.071	20.396	21.794	10.536	
	15.000	20.075	12.410	18.655	14.731	
	10.247	13.856	25.219	16.613	14.142	
	9.592	8.185	19.900	12.923	9.165	
	13.784	13.038	21.237	12.288	9.950	
	5.657	8.775	19.391	10.344	6.633	
	8.000	18.788	13.856	15.330	9.165	
	8.307	19.105	19.596		16.852	
	9.644	20.543			17.117	
Totals	101.327	153.081	174.588	123.080	120.292	$672.367 = \sum X$
Means	10.13	15.31	19.40	15.39	12.03	
S.D.	2.73	5.19	4.00	3.67	3.54	
Var	7.48	26.96	16.03	13.49	12.55	
n	10	10	9	8	10	$47 = N$

11.21 Magnitude of effect for data in Exercise 11.17:

$$\eta^2 = \frac{SS_{group}}{SS_{total}} \qquad\qquad \omega^2 = \frac{SS_{group} - (K-1)MS_{error}}{SS_{total} + MS_{error}}$$

$$= \frac{44.557}{275.839} = .16 \qquad\qquad = \frac{44.557 - (8-1)0.876}{275.839 + 0.876} = .1389$$

11.23 Transforming Time to Speed in Exercise 11.22 involves a reciprocal transformation. The effect of the transformation is to decrease the relative distance between large values.

11.25 The parts of speech (noun vs verb) are fixed. But the individual items within those parts of speech may well be random, representing a random sample of nouns and a random sample of verbs.

> Keep in mind that a random variable is one whose levels you obtain by some sort of random process—such as tossing all possible levels of the independent variable in a hat and drawing out a few. A fixed variable is one you deliberately select. If you wanted to see the effect of recording at different sites in the brain, I suppose that you *could* start stabbing electrodes blindly into the head, and look for differences among the sites in terms of cortical activity. Then Site would be a random variable. I can't imagine why you would want to do that. A better way would be to select half a dozen sites on what you know from reading the literature. Here you are selecting the levels of the independent variable, and you have a fixed model.

11.27 Computer exercise. Reanalysis of data from Exercise 7.41.
The following is SPSS printout.

* * * A N A L Y S I S   O F   V A R I A N C E * * *

         GSIT
    by   GROUP

         UNIQUE sums of squares
         All effects entered simultaneously

Source of Variation	Sum of Squares	DF	Mean Square	F	Sig of F
Main Effects	153.493	2	76.747	.898	.408
GROUP	153.493	2	76.747	.898	.408
Explained	153.493	2	76.747	.898	.408
Residual	31790.736	372	85.459		
Total	31944.229	374	85.412		

381 cases were processed.
6 cases (1.6 pct) were missing.

11.29 Computer exercise. Three one-way ANOVAs for data in Exercise 11.28 broken down by retention interval. These results are from Systat.

```
THE FOLLOWING RESULTS ARE FOR:   INTERVAL    =      1.0000
DEP VAR:  ERRORS      N:     54  MULTIPLE R: 0.714  SQUARED MULTIPLE R: 0.510

                    ANALYSIS OF VARIANCE
SOURCE        SUM-OF-SQUARES   DF  MEAN-SQUARE    F-RATIO        P
DOSAGE          111.0000        2    55.5000     26.5775     0.0000
ERROR           106.5000       51     2.0882

LEAST SQUARES MEANS.
                              LS MEAN       SE       N
     DOSAGE    =    1.0000     3.3333     0.3406     18
     DOSAGE    =    2.0000     5.3333     0.3406     18
     DOSAGE    =    3.0000     1.8333     0.3406     18
****************************************************************

THE FOLLOWING RESULTS ARE FOR:   INTERVAL    =      2.0000

DEP VAR:  ERRORS      N:     36  MULTIPLE R: 0.589  SQUARED MULTIPLE R: 0.347

                    ANALYSIS OF VARIANCE
SOURCE        SUM-OF-SQUARES   DF  MEAN-SQUARE    F-RATIO        P
DOSAGE           32.0556        2    16.0278      8.7787     0.0009
ERROR            60.2500       33     1.8258
```

67

```
LEAST SQUARES MEANS.
                              LS MEAN        SE       N
      DOSAGE    =    1.0000    2.8333      0.3901     12
      DOSAGE    =    2.0000    4.4167      0.3901     12
      DOSAGE    =    3.0000    2.1667      0.3901     12
******************************************************************

THE FOLLOWING RESULTS ARE FOR: INTERVAL     =      3.0000

DEP VAR:  ERRORS      N:     31  MULTIPLE R: 0.455  SQUARED MULTIPLE R: 0.207

                      ANALYSIS OF VARIANCE
SOURCE        SUM-OF-SQUARES    DF    MEAN-SQUARE    F-RATIO        P
DOSAGE           15.6655        2       7.8328       3.6546      0.0389
ERROR            60.0119       28       2.1433

LEAST SQUARES MEANS.
                              LS MEAN        SE       N
      DOSAGE    =    1.0000    3.1667      0.4226     12
      DOSAGE    =    2.0000    4.4167      0.4226     12
      DOSAGE    =    3.0000    2.7143      0.5533      7
```

Group differences decrease over time, although the error term remains approximately constant.

> Note, the purpose of this exercise is to help you see the correspondence between what you already know and computer software. Once you become used to hunting around in the printout for the stuff you want, the process will become clearly and simpler.

11.31 Computer exercise. Repeating Exercise 11.29 for Epineq.dat.

```
THE FOLLOWING RESULTS ARE FOR: INTERVAL     =      1.0000

DEP VAR:  ERRORS      N:     36  MULTIPLE R: 0.689  SQUARED MULTIPLE R: 0.475

                      ANALYSIS OF VARIANCE
SOURCE        SUM-OF-SQUARES    DF    MEAN-SQUARE    F-RATIO        P
DOSAGE           71.7222        2      35.8611      14.9327      0.0000
ERROR            79.2500       33       2.4015

LEAST SQUARES MEANS.           LS MEAN        SE       N
      DOSAGE    =    1.0000    3.1667      0.4474     12
      DOSAGE    =    2.0000    5.3333      0.4474     12
      DOSAGE    =    3.0000    1.9167      0.4474     12
******************************************************************

THE FOLLOWING RESULTS ARE FOR: INTERVAL     =      2.0000

DEP VAR:  ERRORS      N:     36  MULTIPLE R: 0.589  SQUARED MULTIPLE R: 0.347
```

```
                    ANALYSIS OF VARIANCE
SOURCE          SUM-OF-SQUARES   DF   MEAN-SQUARE      F-RATIO        P
DOSAGE             32.0556       2     16.0278         8.7787      0.0009
ERROR              60.2500      33      1.8258

LEAST SQUARES MEANS.               LS MEAN         SE        N
  DOSAGE      =      1.0000         2.8333        0.3901     12
  DOSAGE      =      2.0000         4.4167        0.3901     12
  DOSAGE      =      3.0000         2.1667        0.3901     12
**********************************************************************

THE FOLLOWING RESULTS ARE FOR: INTERVAL      =        3.0000

DEP VAR:  ERRORS      N:      36  MULTIPLE R: 0.565  SQUARED MULTIPLE R: 0.320

                    ANALYSIS OF VARIANCE
SOURCE          SUM-OF-SQUARES   DF   MEAN-SQUARE      F-RATIO        P
DOSAGE             35.0556       2     17.5278         7.7553      0.0017
ERROR              74.5833      33      2.2601

LEAST SQUARES MEANS.               LS MEAN         SE        N
  DOSAGE      =      1.0000         3.1667        0.4340     12
  DOSAGE      =      2.0000         4.4167        0.4340     12
  DOSAGE      =      3.0000         2.0000        0.4340     12
```

11.33 There should be no effect on the magnitude of the data because η^2 is not dependent on the underlying metric of the independent variable.

Chapter 12 Multiple Comparisons Among Treatment Means

12.1 The effects of food and water deprivation on a learning task:

a. ANOVA with linear contrasts:

$T_1 = 90$

$$SS_{total} = \Sigma X^2 - \frac{(\Sigma X)^2}{N}$$

$T_2 = 120$

$$= 6257 - \frac{365^2}{25} = 928.000$$

$T_3 = 40$

$T_4 = 60$

$$SS_{group} = \frac{\Sigma T_j^2}{n} - \frac{(\Sigma X)^2}{N}$$

$T_5 = 55$

$$= \frac{90^2 + \ldots + 55^2}{5} - \frac{365^2}{25} = 816.000$$

$N = 25$

$$SS_{error} = SS_{total} - SS_{group}$$

$n = 5$

$$= 928.000 - 816.000 = 112.000$$

Groups:	ad lib (1)	2/day (2)	food (3)	water (4)	f & w (5)	
Means:	18	24	8	12	11	
a_j:	3	3	-2	-2	-2	$30 = \Sigma a_j^2$
b_j:	1	-1	0	0	0	$2 = \Sigma b_j^2$
c_j:	0	0	1	1	-2	$6 = \Sigma c_j^2$
d_j:	0	0	1	-1	0	$2 = \Sigma d_j^2$

$$L_1 = \Sigma a_j \overline{X}_j = (3)(18) + (3)(24) + (-2)(8) + (-2)(12) + (-2)(11) = 64$$

$$L_2 = \Sigma b_j \overline{X}_j = (1)(18) + (-1)(24) + (0)(8) + (0)(12) + (0)(11) = -6$$

$$L_3 = \Sigma c_j \overline{X}_j = (0)(18) + (0)(24) + (1)(8) + (1)(12) + (-2)(11) = -2$$

$$L_3 = \Sigma d_j \overline{X}_j = (0)(18) + (0)(24) + (1)(8) + (-1)(12) + (0)(11) = -4$$

$$SS_{contrast_1} = \frac{nL^2}{\Sigma a_j^2} = \frac{5(64)^2}{30} = 862.667$$

$$SS_{contrast_2} = \frac{nL^2}{\Sigma b_j^2} = \frac{5(-6)^2}{2} = 90.000$$

$$SS_{contrast_3} = \frac{nL^2}{\Sigma c_j^2} = \frac{5(-2)^2}{6} = 3.333$$

$$SS_{contrast_4} = \frac{nL^2}{\Sigma d_j^2} = \frac{5(-4)^2}{2} = 40.000$$

Source	df	SS	MS	F
Deprivation	4	816.000	204.000	36.429*
1&2 vs 3,4,5	1	682.667	682.667	121.905*
1 vs 2	1	90.000	90.000	16.071*
3&4 vs 5	1	3.333	3.333	<1
3 vs 4	1	40.000	40.000	7.143*
Error	20	112.000	5.600	
Total	24	928.000		

$*p < .05$ $[F_{.05(4,20)} = 2.87 ; F_{.05(1,20)} = 4.35]$

b. Orthogonality of contrasts:

Cross-products of coefficients:

$$\Sigma a_j b_j = (3)(1) + (3)(-1) + (-2)(0) + (-2)(0) + (-2)(0) = 0$$

$$\Sigma a_j c_j = (3)(0) + (3)(0) + (-2)(1) + (-2)(1) + (-2)(-2) = 0$$

$$\Sigma a_j d_j = (3)(0) + (3)(0) + (-2)(1) + (-2)(-1) + (-2)(0) = 0$$

$$\Sigma b_j c_j = (1)(0) + (-1)(0) + (0)(1) + (0)(1) + (0)(-2) = 0$$

$$\Sigma c_j d_j = (0)(0) + (0)(0) + (1)(1) + (1)(-1) + (-2)(0) = 0$$

c. $SS_{treat} = \Sigma SS_{contrast}$

$816.000 = 682.667 + 90.000 + 3.333 + 40.000$

71

> Keep in mind that to create a set of contrasts, you use the number of groups on each side of the contrast as the coefficients for the other set of groups. That's why Ad Lib Control and 2/Day Control have coefficients of 3; they are being compared against the combination of three other groups.
>
> To show that sets of coefficients are orthogonal, we just show that their cross-products sum to 0.0. Finally, if the contrasts are orthogonal, and if we have as many contrasts as degrees of freedom, their sums of squares must sum to SS_{treat}.

12.3 For $\alpha = .05$:

Per comparison error rate $= \alpha = .05$
Familywise error rate $= 1 - (1 - \alpha)^2 = .0975$.

> If contrasts were not orthogonal, we couldn't calculate the familywise error rate based on what we know. But it would most likely be close to .0975. It certainly would never be less than .05 nor more than $2(.05) = .10$

12.5 Studentized range statistic for data in Exercise 11.2:

$$\overline{X}_1 = 19.3 \quad n_1 = 10$$

$$\overline{X}_2 = 12.0 \quad n_2 = 10$$

$$q_2 = \frac{\overline{X}_1 - \overline{X}_2}{\sqrt{\dfrac{MS_{error}}{n}}} = \frac{19.3 - 12.0}{\sqrt{\dfrac{10.56}{10}}} = \frac{7.3}{1.028} = 7.101$$

$$q_2 = 7.10 = 5.023\sqrt{2} = 7.10 = t\sqrt{2}$$

12.7 The Bonferroni test on contrasts in Exercise 12.2 (data from Exercise 11.1):

From Exercise 12.2: $L_1 = -30.00$ $\quad$ $L_2 = -20.00$ $\quad$ $n = 6$

$$\Sigma a_j^2 = 6 \qquad \Sigma b_j^2 = 2 \qquad MS_{error} = 26.167$$

$$t' = \frac{L}{\sqrt{\dfrac{\Sigma a_j^2 MS_{error}}{n}}} \qquad t_1' = \frac{-30.00}{\sqrt{\dfrac{6(26.167)}{6}}} = -5.86 \quad t_2' = \frac{-20.00}{\sqrt{\dfrac{2(26.167)}{6}}} = -6.77$$

$[t'_{.05}(df_{error} = 15; 2 \text{ comparisons}) = 2.49]$ $\qquad$ Reject H_0 in each case.

12.9 Holm's multistage test for data in Exercise 12.1.

Comparison	F	t	c	$t'_{.05(20,c)}$	Signif
1&2 vs 3,4,5	121.905	11.04	4	2.74	*
1 vs. 2	16.071	4.01	3	2.61	*
3 vs. 4	7.143	2.67	2	2.42	*
3&4 vs. 5	<1	<1	1	2.09	

Reject the first three null hypotheses but not the fourth. If this had been a standard Bonferroni test we would have rejected only the first two null hypotheses.

> Once again, we are changing the critical value, not the calculations.

12.11 Tukey's test on example in Table 11.2 (page 308):

Tukey's test is the same as the Newman-Keuls test except that the first (most conservative) q_r is taken as the critical value for all comparisons, and denoted q_{HSD}.

Group	Rhyme	Count	Adj	Intent	Image		r		q_{HSD}		W_r
Means	6.9	7.0	11	12	13.4						
Rhyme	--	0.1	4.1	5.1	6.5	...	5	...	4.04	...	3.973
Count		--	4.0	5.0	6.4	...	4	...	4.04	...	3.973
Adj			--	1.0	2.4	...	3	...	4.04	...	3.973
Intent				--	1.4	...	2	...	4.04	...	3.973
Image					--						

Significance

Group:	Rhyme	Count	Adj	Intent	Image
Means:	6.9	7.0	11.0	12.0	13.4
Rhyme			*	*	*
Count			*	*	*
Adj					
Intent					
Image					

The counting and imagery groups are homogeneous, but are different from the adjective, intentional, and rhyming conditions, which are also homogeneous. This is the same pattern of differences that we found with the Newman-Keuls.

12.13 For Tukey's HSD test:

Table (1), (2), and (4) are the same as found in Exercise 12.12. In (3) the values are based on df' and $r = 4$.

(3) Matrix of q_{HSD}:

Group:	1	2	3	4	5
1	--	4.89	4.41	4.45	4.37
2		--	4.76	4.89	4.76
3			--	4.45	4.37
4				--	4.41
5					--

The critical values are not constant because df' varies. All are taken at $r = 5$.

(5) Matrix of W_r = product of corresponding elements of (3) & (4):

Group:	1	2	3	4	5
1	--	5.67	4.41	4.41	4.33
2		--	5.66	5.77	5.66
3			--	4.58	4.50
4				--	4.50
5					--

The same pattern of significance is found as in Exercise 12.12.

12.15 Tukey's HSD test applied to the THC data in Table 11.4 (p. 320).

The variances are approximately equal, and so are the sample sizes, so we will use the harmonic mean of the n_j.

Group:	1	2	3	4	5
μg THC	0	0.1	0.5	1	2
n_j	10	10	9	8	10

$$n_h = \frac{k}{\Sigma(\frac{1}{n_j})} = \frac{5}{\frac{1}{10} + \frac{1}{10} + \frac{1}{9} + \frac{1}{8} + \frac{1}{10}} = 9.326$$

Group	1	5	4	2	3		r		q_{HSD}		W_r
Means	34.00	38.10	18.50	50.80	60.33						
1	--	4.1	14.5	16.8	26.33*	...	5	...	4.04	...	20.51
5		--	10.4	12.7	22.23*	...	4	...	4.04	...	20.51
4			--	2.3	11.83	...	3	...	4.04	...	20.51
2				--	9.53	...	2	...	4.04	...	20.51
3					--						

$$w_r = q_{.05}(r, df) \sqrt{\frac{MS_{error}}{\overline{N}_h}} = 4.04 \sqrt{\frac{240.35}{9.326}} = 20.51$$

The 0.5μg group is different from the control group and the 2μg group. All other differences are not significant. The maximum familywise error rate is .05.

> This procedure is more complicated because we have to take into account the varying sample sizes. Thus we calculate the harmonic mean of the sample sizes, and then use that to calculate W_r. This works just fine unless we have very different sample sizes.
>
> The maximum familywise error rate here is .05, because Tukey always holds the maximum familywise error rate at whatever α you choose.

12.17 If you are willing to sacrifice using a common error term, you simply run the relevant *t* tests but evaluate them at $\alpha' = \alpha / c$.

12.19 Linear and quadratic trend in Conti and Musty (1984).

The results given below assume that you have added the three observations mentioned in the exercise.

Group:	Control	0.1	0.5	1	2	
Means:	34.00	50.80	60.33	48.50	38.10	
Linear	-0.72	-0.62	-0.22	0.28	1.28	$\Sigma a_j^2 = 2.668$
Quadratic	0.389	0.199	-0.362	-0.612	0.387	$\Sigma b_j^2 = 0.846$

$$L_{Linear} = \Sigma a_j \overline{X}_j = -.72(34.00) - .62(50.80) - .22(60.33) + .28(48.50)$$

$$+ 1.28(38.10) = -6.901$$

75

$$L_{Quad} = \Sigma b_j \, \overline{X}_j = .389(34.00) + .199(50.80) - .362(60.33)$$

$$- .612(48.50) + .387(38.10) = -13.44$$

$$SS_{Linear} = \frac{nL^2}{\Sigma a_j^2} = \frac{10(-6.901^2)}{2.668} = 178.479$$

$$SS_{Quad} = \frac{nL^2}{\Sigma b_j^2} = \frac{10(-13.44^2)}{.846} = 2135.645$$

Source	df	SS	MS	F
Treatments	4	4396.12	1099.03	4.90*
Linear	1	178.48	178.48	<1
Quadratic	1	2135.64	2135.64	9.52*
Error	45	10095.10	224.34	
Total	49	14491.22		

$*p < .05 \quad [F_{.05(4,45)} = 2.58; F_{.05(1,45)} = 4.06]$

There is a significant quadratic trend, but no significant linear trend. This quadratic trend is clearly visible in the means.

> For an example like this where the levels of the independent variable vary along an interval scale, you probably learn more from looking at trend components than you do looking at individual group differences, because you usually want to see that the dependent variable increases and then decreased as you move across levels of the independent variable, rather than worrying specifically about which groups are different from which other groups.

12.21 Computer example.

12.23 Trend analysis for Epineq.dat separately at each interval.

One Day: $F_{Linear} = 9.44$ (p = .0042); $F_{Quad} = 20.43$ (p = .0001)

One Week: $F_{Linear} = 4.33$ (p = .0453); $F_{Quad} = 13.23$ (p = .0009)

One Month: $F_{Linear} = 6.91$ (p = .0129); $F_{Quad} = 8.60$ (p = .0061)

Although it can be difficult to derive the trend coefficients by hand for such a problem, many software statistical packages will solve for the trend components without your having to supply the coefficients.

Chapter 13 - Factorial Analysis of Variance

13.1 Mother/infant interaction for primiparous/multiparous mothers under or over 18 years of age with LBW or full-term infants:

		Size/Age			
		LBW < 18	LBW > 18	NBW	
Mother's Parity	Primi-	45	53	64	162
	Multi-	39	69	82	190
		84	122	146	352 = ΣX

$\Sigma X^2 = 2404$

$N = 60$

$n = 10$

$p = 2 \quad s = 3$

$$SS_{total} = \Sigma X^2 - \frac{(\Sigma X)^2}{N} = 2404 - \frac{352^2}{60} = 338.93$$

$$SS_P = \frac{\Sigma T_P^2}{sn} - \frac{(\Sigma X)^2}{N} \qquad\qquad SS_S = \frac{\Sigma T_S^2}{pn} - \frac{(\Sigma X)^2}{N}$$

$$= \frac{162^2 + 190^2}{3(10)} - \frac{352^2}{60} \qquad\qquad = \frac{84^2 + 122^2 + 146^2}{2(10)} - \frac{352^2}{60}$$

$$= 13.067 \qquad\qquad\qquad\qquad = 97.733$$

$$SS_{cells} = \frac{\Sigma T_{cell}^2}{n} - \frac{(\Sigma X)^2}{N}$$

$$= \frac{45^2 + 53^2 + 64^2 + 39^2 + 69^2 + 82^2}{10} - \frac{352^2}{60} = 128.53$$

$$SS_{PS} = SS_{cells} - SS_P - SS_S = 128.53 - 13.067 - 97.733 = 17.733$$

$$SS_{error} = SS_{total} - SS_{cells} = 338.93 - 128.53 = 210.40$$

Source	df	SS	MS	F
Parity	1	13.067	13.067	3.354
Size/Age	2	97.733	48.867	12.541*
P x S	2	17.733	8.867	2.276
Error	54	210.400	3.896	
Total	59	338.933		

*$p < .05 \quad [F_{.05(2,54)} = 3.17]$

13.3 The mean for these primiparous mothers would not be expected to be a good estimate of the mean for the population of all primiparous mothers because 50% of the population of primiparous mothers do not give birth to LBW infants. This would be important if we wished to take means from this sample as somehow representing the population means for primiparous and multiparous mothers.

13.5 Memory of avoidance of a fear-producing stimulus:

		Area of Stimulation			
		Neutral	Area A	Area B	
	50	143	84	122	349
Delay	100	140	115	80	335
	150	140	134	132	406
		423	333	334	$1090 = \Sigma X$

$\Sigma X^2 = 28374$ $N = 45$ $n = 5$ $a = 3$ $d = 3$

$$SS_{total} = \Sigma X^2 - \frac{(\Sigma X)^2}{N} = 28374 - \frac{1090^2}{45} = 1971.778$$

$$SS_D = \frac{\Sigma T_D^2}{an} - \frac{(\Sigma X)^2}{N}$$

$$= \frac{349^2 + 335^2 + 406^2}{3(5)} - \frac{1090^2}{45} = 188.578$$

$$SS_A = \frac{\Sigma T_A^2}{dn} - \frac{(\Sigma X)^2}{N}$$

$$= \frac{423^2 + 333^2 + 334^2}{3(5)} - \frac{1090^2}{45} = 356.044$$

$$SS_{cells} = \frac{\Sigma T^2_{cell}}{n} - \frac{(\Sigma X)^2}{N}$$

$$= \frac{143^2 + 84^2 + \ldots + 132^2}{5} - \frac{268^2}{45} = 916.578$$

$$SS_{DA} = SS_{cells} - SS_D - SS_A = 916.578 - 188.578 - 356.044 = 371.956$$

$$SS_{error} = SS_{total} - SS_{cells} = 1971.778 - 916.578 = 1055.200$$

Source	df	SS	MS	F
Delay	2	188.578	94.289	3.22
Area	2	356.044	178.022	6.07*
D x A	4	371.956	92.989	3.17*
Error	36	1055.200	29.311	
Total	44	1971.778		

$*p < .05 \quad [F_{.05(2,36)} = 3.27; F_{.05(4,36)} = 2.64]$

13.7 In Exercise 13.5, if A refers to Area:

$\hat{\alpha}_1$ = the treatment effect for the Neutral site

$$= \overline{X}.. - \overline{X}._1$$

$$= 24.222 - 28.2$$

$$= 3.9778$$

> Remember that the treatment effect is the degree to which that the mean of the treatment deviates from the overall population mean.

13.9 The Bonferroni test to compare Site means.

$$t = \frac{\overline{N} - \overline{A}}{\sqrt{\frac{MS_{error}}{n_N} + \frac{MS_{error}}{n_A}}} \qquad t = \frac{\overline{N} - \overline{B}}{\sqrt{\frac{MS_{error}}{n_N} + \frac{MS_{error}}{n_B}}}$$

$$= \frac{28.20 - 22.20}{\sqrt{\frac{29.311}{15} + \frac{29.311}{15}}} \qquad = \frac{28.20 - 22.27}{\sqrt{\frac{29.311}{15} + \frac{29.311}{15}}}$$

$$= 3.03 \ (\text{Reject } H_0) \qquad = 3.00 \ (\text{Reject } H_0)$$

$[t'_{.025}(2,36) = \pm 2.34]$

We can conclude that both the difference between Groups N and A and between Groups N and B are significant, and our familywise error rate will not exceed $\alpha = .05$.

13.11 Rerunning Exercise 11.3 as a factorial design:

The following printout is from Systat.

```
DEP VAR:  RECALL      N:     40  MULTIPLE R: 0.903  SQUARED MULTIPLE R: 0.816
                     ANALYSIS OF VARIANCE
SOURCE         SUM-OF-SQUARES   DF   MEAN-SQUARE      F-RATIO       P
AGE                115.6000      1     115.6000       17.4417     0.0002
LEVEL             792.1000      1     792.1000      119.5122     0.0000
AGE*LEVEL         152.1000      1     152.1000       22.9489     0.0000
ERROR             238.6000     36       6.6278
```

Cell means

AGE	=	1.0000			
LEVEL	=	1.0000	6.5000	0.8141	10
AGE	=	1.0000			
LEVEL	=	2.0000	19.3000	0.8141	10
AGE	=	2.0000			
LEVEL	=	1.0000	7.0000	0.8141	10
AGE	=	2.0000			
LEVEL	=	2.0000	12.0000	0.8141	10

The results show that there is a significance difference between younger and older subjects, that there is better recall in tasks which require more processing, and that there is an interaction between age and level of processing. The difference between the two levels of processing is greater for the younger subjects than it is for the older ones, primarily because the older ones do not do much better with greater amounts of processing.

> This is a nice illustration of the fact that a factorial design, when appropriate, can give you more information that two one-way analyses (or one larger one-way) Notice the relationship between the sums of squares you found in Exercise 11.3 and the Location effect here. (That is the focus of the next exercise. It's worth looking closely to see what is the the same and what is different.)

13.13 Made-up data with main effects but no interaction:

Cell means: 8   12

                  4   6

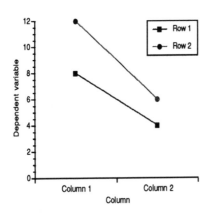

13.15 The interaction was of primary interest in an experiment by Nisbett in which he showed that obese people varied the amount of food they consumed depending on whether a lot or a little food was visible, while normal weight subjects ate approximately the same amount under the two conditions.

13.17 Unequal sample sizes in hospital patients responses to two different therapies:

Cell Totals: Treatment

		A	B	
Hospital	#1	19	66	85
	#2	22	109	131
		41	175	$216 = \Sigma X$

Cell ns: Treatment

		A	B	
Hospital	#1	3	6	9
	#2	2	4	6
		5	10	$15 = \Sigma X$

$$\overline{N}_h = \frac{k}{\Sigma \frac{1}{n_i}} = \frac{4}{\frac{1}{3} + \frac{1}{6} + \frac{1}{2} + \frac{1}{4}} = 3.2$$

Cell Means:

		Treatment		
		A	B	
Hospital	#1	6.33	11.00	8.665
	#2	11.00	27.25	19.125
		8.665	19.125	13.895 = ΣX

Adj Cell Totals:

		Treatment		
		A	B	
Hospital	#1	20.256	35.200	55.456
	#2	35.200	87.200	122.400
		55.456	122.400	177.856 = ΣX(adj)

$$SS_H = \frac{\Sigma T_H^2}{t\bar{n}_h} - \frac{(\Sigma X)^2}{ht\bar{n}_h}$$

$$= \frac{55.456^2 + 122.4^2}{2(3.2)} - \frac{177.856^2}{2(2)(3.2)} = 350.117$$

$$SS_T = \frac{\Sigma T_T^2}{h\bar{n}_h} - \frac{(\Sigma X)^2}{ht\bar{n}_h}$$

$$= \frac{55.456^2 + 122.4^2}{2(3.2)} - \frac{177.856^2}{2(2)(3.2)} = 350.117$$

$$SS_{cells} = \frac{\Sigma T_{cells}^2}{\bar{n}_h} - \frac{(\Sigma X)^2}{ht\bar{n}_h}$$

$$= \frac{20.256^2 + 35.2^2 + \ldots + 87.200^2}{3.2} - \frac{177.856^2}{2(2)(3.2)} = 807.429$$

$$SS_{HT} = SS_{cells} - SS_H - SS_T = 807.429 - 350.117 - 350.117 = 107.195$$

Cell variances:

		Treatment	
		A	B
Hospital	#1	2.333	4.400
	#2	2.000	72.917

$$SS_{error} = \Sigma(n_{ij} - 1)s_{ij}^2 = 2(2.333) + 5(4.400) + 1(2.000) + 3(72.917) = 247.417$$

Source	df	SS	MS	F
Hospital	1	350.117	350.117	15.57*
Therapy	1	350.117	350.117	15.57*
H X T	1	107.195	107.195	4.77
Error	11	247.417	22.492	
Total	14			

$*p < .05$ $[F_{.05(1,11)} = 4.84]$

We can conclude that there are effects due to both Hospital and Therapy, but there is no interaction between the two main effect variables. (Notice the heterogeneity of variance.)

It is instructive to compare this result (which produces equal effects for rows and columns) with the result that we would achieve if we just took the average of the observations in the rows (or columns). If we did that we would see that the difference between the row means (9.44 and 21.83) is more than the difference we would find between the column means (8.2 and 17.5).

> If you recognize that these cell frequencies have the property that I defined as "proportionality," you might be tempted to divide each squared total by its own n as you go along. If you did that, you would get quite a different summary table. You would effectively be comparing weighted means with such an analysis. But you would only do that if you had a reason why you were willing to compare weighted means (an unlikely need) and wanted to let the sample sizes play a direct role in the outcome.

13.19 Magnitude of effect for mother-infant interaction data in Exercise 13.2:

$$\eta_P^2 = \frac{SS_{parity}}{SS_{total}} = \frac{13.067}{338.933} = .04$$

$$\eta_S^2 = \frac{SS_{size}}{SS_{total}} = \frac{97.733}{338.933} = .29$$

$$\eta_{PS}^2 = \frac{SS_{PS}}{SS_{total}} = \frac{17.733}{338.933} = .05$$

$$\omega_P^2 = \frac{SS_{parity} - (p-1)MS_{error}}{SS_{total} + MS_{error}} = \frac{13.067 - (1)(3.896)}{338.933 + 3.896} = .03$$

$$\omega_S^2 = \frac{SS_{size} - (s-1)MS_{error}}{SS_{total} + MS_{error}} = \frac{97.733 - (2)(3.896)}{338.933 + 3.896} = .26$$

$$\omega_{PS}^2 = \frac{SS_{PS} - (p-1)(s-1)MS_{error}}{SS_{total} + MS_{error}} = \frac{17.733 - (1)(2)(3.896)}{338.933 + 3.896} = .03$$

13.21 Three-way ANOVA on Early Experience x Intensity of UCS x Conditioned Stimulus (Tone or Vibration):

E×I×C Cells	CS = Tone				CS = Vibration				
Experience:	High	Med	Low		High	Med	Low		
Control	11	16	21	48	19	24	29	72	120
Tone	25	28	34	87	21	26	31	78	165
Vib	6	13	20	39	40	41	52	133	172
Both	22	30	30	82	35	38	48	121	203
	64	87	105	256	115	129	160	404	660

E×I Cells	Intensity			
Experience:	High	Med	Low	
Control	30	40	50	120
Tone	46	54	65	165
Vib	46	54	72	172
Both	57	68	78	203
	179	216	265	660

E×C Cells	Cond Stimulus		
Experience:	Tone	Vib	
Control	48	72	120
Tone	87	78	165
Vib	39	133	172
Both	82	121	203
	256	404	660

I×C Cells	Cond Stim		
Intensity:	Tone	Vib	
High	64	115	179
Med	87	129	216
Low	105	160	265
	256	404	660

$$SS_{Exp} = \frac{\Sigma T_e^2}{nic} - \frac{(\Sigma X)^2}{N} = \frac{120^2 + 165^2 + 172^2 + 203^2}{5(3)(2)} - \frac{660^2}{120} = 117.267$$

$$SS_{Int} = \frac{\Sigma T_i^2}{nec} - \frac{(\Sigma X)^2}{N} = \frac{179^2 + 216^2 + 265^2}{5(4)(2)} - \frac{660^2}{120} = 93.050$$

$$SS_{CS} = \frac{\Sigma T_c^2}{nei} - \frac{(\Sigma X)^2}{N} = \frac{256^2 + 404^2}{5(4)(3)} - \frac{660^2}{120} = 182.533$$

$$SS_{cells_{EI}} = \frac{\Sigma T_{cells_{EI}}^2}{nc} - \frac{(\Sigma X)^2}{N} = \frac{30^2 + 40^2 + \ldots + 78^2}{5(2)} - \frac{660^2}{120} = 213.000$$

$$SS_{EI} = SS_{cells_{EI}} - SS_{Exp} - SS_{Int} = 213.000 - 117.267 - 93.050 = 2.683$$

$$SS_{cells_{EC}} = \frac{\Sigma T_{cells_{EC}}^2}{ni} - \frac{(\Sigma X)^2}{N} = \frac{48^2 + 72^2 + \ldots + 121^2}{5(3)} - \frac{660^2}{120} = 484.400$$

$$SS_{EC} = SS_{cells_{EC}} - SS_{Exp} - SS_{CS} = 484.400 - 117.267 - 182.533 = 184.600$$

$$SS_{cells_{IC}} = \frac{\Sigma T_{cells_{IC}}^2}{ne} - \frac{(\Sigma X)^2}{N} = \frac{64^2 + 115^2 + \ldots + 160^2}{5(4)} - \frac{660^2}{120} = 277.800$$

$$SS_{IC} = SS_{cells_{IC}} - SS_{Int} - SS_{CS} = 277.800 - 93.050 - 182.533 = 2.217$$

$$SS_{cells_{EIC}} = \frac{\Sigma T_{cells_{EIC}}^2}{n} - \frac{(\Sigma X)^2}{N} = \frac{11^2 + 16^2 + \ldots + 48^2}{5} - \frac{660^2}{120} = 587.200$$

$$SS_{EIC} = SS_{cells_{EIC}} - SS_{Exp} - SS_{Int} - SS_{CS} - SS_{EI} - SS_{EC} - SS_{IC}$$
$$= 587.200 - 117.267 - 93.050 - 182.533 - 2.683 - 184.600 - 2.217$$
$$= 4.850$$

$$SS_{error} = SS_{total} - SS_{cells_{EIC}} = 1646.000 - 587.200 = 1058.800$$

Source	df	SS	MS	F
Experience	3	117.267	39.089	3.544*
Intensity	2	93.050	46.525	4.218*
Cond Stim	1	182.533	182.533	16.550*
E x I	6	2.683	0.447	<1
E x C	3	184.600	61.533	5.579*
I x C	2	2.217	1.108	<1
E x I x C	6	4.850	0.808	<1
Error	96	1058.800	11.029	
Total	119	1646.000		

$*p < .05 \quad [F_{.05(1,96)} = 3.94; F_{.05(2,96)} = 3.09; F_{.05(3,96)} = 2.70; F_{.05(6,96)} = 2.19]$

There are significant main effects for all variables with a significant Experience $\times$ Conditioned Stimulus interaction.

> Notice that you were able to solve this problem given only the cell totals and SS_{total}. But that means that you could also solve the problem if I had given you the cell means and the overall variance, or the cell means and the cell standard deviations. (Just average the squared standard deviations to get MS_{error}.) Means and standard deviations are very frequently included in research results.

13.23 Computer exercise.

13.25 The average of the nine within-cell variances will equal MS_{error} (2.162) in Exercise 13.24.

> This goes back to what I said after Exercise 13.19. The error term is the average within-cell variance.

13.27 Three-way analysis of variance for Tab13-12.dat.

Source	df	SS	MS	F
Experience	1	1302.083	1302.083	48.78*
Road	2	1016.667	508.333	19.04*
Exper*Road	2	116.667	58.333	2.19
Condition	1	918.750	918.750	34.42*
Exper*Cond	1	216.750	216.750	8.12*
Road*Cond	2	50.000	25.000	0.94
Exper*Road*Cond	2	146.000	73.000	2.73
Error	36	961.000	26.694	
Total	47	4727.917		

13.29 If in fact we think that males are generally more optimistic than females, then the sample sizes themselves are part of the "treatment" effect. We probably would not want to ignore that if we are looking a sex as an independent variable. In fact, the lack of independence between sample size and the effect under study is an important problem when it occurs.

> This is one reason why I encourage you to design studies with equal sample sizes. Even if things don't work out and you have some missing data, the data will probably not be missing systematically, and the results will be meaningful.
>
> This is also one of the reasons why most researchers much prefer "experiments" where the experimenter creates the groups and conditions, over observational (field) studies where we take our samples as we find them.

Chapter 14 - Repeated Measures Designs

14.1 Does taking the GRE repeatedly lead to higher scores?

    a. Statistical model:

$$X_{ij} = \mu + \pi_i + \tau_j + \pi\tau_{ij} + e_{ij} \text{ or } X_{ij} = \mu + \pi_i + \tau_j + e_{ij}'$$

    b. Analysis:

Subject	Total
1	1700
2	1350
3	1850
4	1990
5	1310
6	2090
7	1510
8	1720
Total	13520 = ΣX

$\Sigma X^2 = 7811200$

$N = 24$

$s = 8$

$t = 3$

Test Session	Total
1	4420
2	4510
3	4590

$$SS_{total} = \Sigma X^2 - \frac{(\Sigma X)^2}{N}$$

$$= 7811200 - \frac{(13520)^2}{24} = 194933.33$$

$$SS_{subj} = \frac{\Sigma T_s^2}{t} - \frac{(\Sigma X)^2}{N}$$

$$= \frac{(1700)^2 + \ldots + (1720)^2}{3} - \frac{(13520)^2}{24} = 18966.66$$

$$SS_{test} = \frac{\Sigma T_t^2}{s} - \frac{(\Sigma X)^2}{N}$$

$$= \frac{(4420)^2 + (4510)^2 + (4590)^2}{8} - \frac{(13520)^2}{24} = 1808.33$$

$$SS_{error} = SS_{total} - SS_{subj} - SS_{test}$$

$$= 194933.33 - 189666.66 - 1808.33 = 3458.33$$

Source	df	SS	MS	F
Subjects	7	189666.66		
Within Subj	16	5266.67		
Test Session	2	1808.33	904.17	3.66 ns
Error	14	3458.33	247.02	
Total	23	194933.33		

$[F_{.05(2,14)} = 3.74]$

> Notice the sum of squares for Subjects in this table. It is an indication of how much "error" variability you were able to remove by making using repeated measures and subjects a factor in your design.

14.3 Teaching of self-care skills to severely retarded children:

Cell totals:

		Phase		
		Baseline	Training	Total
Group:	Exp	48	70	118
	Control	47	64	111
	Total	95	134	229

Subject totals:

		S_1	S_2	S_3	S_4	S_5	S_6	S_7	S_8	S_9	S_{10}
Group:	Exp	17	12	5	12	11	13	13	11	11	13
	Control	8	10	18	7	8	16	15	9	10	10

$\Sigma X^2 = 1501 \quad N = 40 \quad n = 10 \quad g = 2 \quad p = 2$

$$SS_{total} = \Sigma X^2 - \frac{(\Sigma X)^2}{N} = 1501 - \frac{(229)^2}{40} = 189.975$$

$$SS_{Subjects} = \frac{\Sigma T_{Subjects}^2}{p} - \frac{(\Sigma X)^2}{N} = \frac{17^2 + 12^2 + \ldots + 10^2}{2} - \frac{229^2}{40} = 106.475$$

$$SS_{Groups} = \frac{\Sigma T_G^2}{pn} - \frac{(\Sigma X)^2}{N} = \frac{118^2 + 111^2}{2(10)} - \frac{229^2}{40} = 1.225$$

$$SS_{Phases} = \frac{\Sigma T_P^2}{gn} - \frac{(\Sigma X)^2}{N} = \frac{95^2 + 134^2}{2(10)} - \frac{229^2}{40} = 38.025$$

$$SS_{Cells} = \frac{\Sigma T_C^2}{n} - \frac{(\Sigma X)^2}{N} = \frac{48^2 + 70^2 + 47^2 + 64^2}{10} - \frac{229^2}{40} = 39.875$$

$$SS_{PG} = SS_{Cells} - SS_{Phase} - SS_{Groups} = 39.875 - 38.025 - 1.225 = 0.625$$

Source	df	SS	MS	F
Between Subj	19	106.475		
Groups	1	1.125	1.125 <1	
Ss w/in Grps	18	105.250	5.847	
Within Subj	20	83.500		
Phase	1	38.025	38.025	15.26*
P x G	1	0.625	0.625 <1 = 0.25	
P x Ss w/in Grps	18	44.850	2.492	
Total	39	189.975		

*$p < .05$ $[F_{.05(1,18)} = 4.41]$

There is a significant difference between baseline and training, but there are no group differences nor a group x phase interaction.

> There is a difference between baseline and training, but no group differences and no interaction. That probably suggests that we are observing changes over time that have nothing to do with our training, though it may have to do with the extra attention the students receive. If training were important, we would *at least* expect to see an interaction, with a greater change in the Training condition than in the Control condition.

14.5   Adding a No Attention control group to the study in Exercise 14.3:

Cell totals:

		Phase		
		Baseline	Training	Total
	Exp	48	70	118
Group:	Att Cont	47	64	111
	No Att Cont	51	46	97
	Total	146	180	326

Subject totals:

		S_1	S_2	S_3	S_4	S_5	S_6	S_7	S_8	S_9	S_{10}
	Exp	17	12	5	12	11	13	13	11	11	13
Group:	Att Cont	8	10	18	7	8	16	15	9	10	10
	No Att Cont	7	10	14	11	9	13	13	9	5	6

$\Sigma X^2 = 2026$ $N = 60$ $n = 10$ $g = 3$ $p = 2$

$$SS_{Total} = \Sigma X^2 - \frac{(\Sigma X)^2}{N} = 2026 - \frac{(326)^2}{40} = 254.7333$$

$$SS_{Subjects} = \frac{\Sigma T^2_{Subjects}}{p} - \frac{(\Sigma X)^2}{N} = \frac{17^2 + 12^2 + \ldots + 6^2}{2} - \frac{326^2}{60} = 159.7333$$

$$SS_{Groups} = \frac{\Sigma T^2_G}{pn} - \frac{(\Sigma X)^2}{N} = \frac{118^2 + 111^2 + 97^2}{2(10)} - \frac{326^2}{60} = 11.4333$$

$$SS_{Phases} = \frac{\Sigma T^2_P}{gn} - \frac{(\Sigma X)^2}{N} = \frac{146^2 + 180^2}{3(10)} - \frac{326^2}{60} = 19.2667$$

$$SS_{Cells} = \frac{\Sigma T^2_C}{n} - \frac{(\Sigma X)^2}{N} = \frac{48^2 + 70^2 + \ldots + 46^2}{10} - \frac{326^2}{60} = 52.3333$$

$$SS_{PG} = SS_{Cells} - SS_{Phase} - SS_{Groups} = 51.3333 - 11.4333 - 19.2667 = 20.6333$$

Source	df	SS	MS	F
Between Subj	29	159.7333		
Groups	2	11.4333	5.7166	1.04
Ss w/ Grps	27	148.3000	5.4926	
Within Subj	30	95.0000		
Phase	1	19.2667	19.2667	9.44*
P * G	2	20.6333	10.3165	5.06*
P * Ss w/Grps	27	55.1000	2.0407	
Total	59	254.7333		

$*p < .05 \quad [F_{.05(1,27)} = 4.22; F_{.05(2,27)} = 3.36]$

b. Plot:

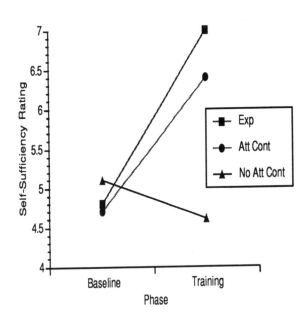

c. There seems to be no difference between the Experimental and Attention groups, but both show significantly more improvement than the No Attention group.

Here we can see that apparently attention played a role. The two attention groups increased approximately the same amount, as we know from Exercise 14.3, but the no attention group did not improve. (In fact, it decreased slightly.) You see here a good example of why we much prefer studies that contain an untreated control group.

14.7 For the data in Exercise 14.6:

a. Variance-covariance matrices:

$$\hat{\Sigma}_{owners} = \begin{bmatrix} 1.30 & 1.50 & 0.75 \\ 1.50 & 2.00 & 1.00 \\ 0.75 & 1.00 & 1.00 \end{bmatrix}$$

$$\hat{\Sigma}_{non\text{-}owners} = \begin{bmatrix} 2.70 & 1.20 & 1.85 \\ 1.20 & 0.70 & 0.60 \\ 1.85 & 0.60 & 3.30 \end{bmatrix}$$

$$\hat{\Sigma}_{pooled} = \begin{bmatrix} 2.00 & 1.35 & 1.30 \\ 1.35 & 1.35 & 0.80 \\ 1.30 & 0.80 & 2.15 \end{bmatrix} \quad \begin{matrix} \bar{s}_j \\ 1.550 \\ 1.167 \\ 1.417 \end{matrix}$$

92

$$\hat{\Sigma}_{between} = \begin{bmatrix} 4.50 & 9.00 & 34.50 \\ 9.00 & 18.00 & 69.00 \\ 34.50 & 69.00 & 264.50 \end{bmatrix}$$

b. $\hat{e}$:

$$\bar{s}_{jj} = \frac{2.00 + 1.35 + 2.15}{3} = 1.833$$

$$\bar{s} = \frac{2.00 + \dots + 2.15}{9} = 1.378$$

$$\Sigma s_{jk}^2 = 2.00^2 + \dots + 2.15^2 = 18.750$$

$$\Sigma \bar{s}_j^2 = 1.550^2 + 1.167^2 + 1.417^2 = 5.772$$

$$\hat{e} = \frac{b^2(\bar{s}_{jj} - \bar{s})^2}{(b-1)(\Sigma s_{jk}^2 - 2b\Sigma\bar{s}_j^2 + b^2\bar{s}^2)} = \frac{9(1.833 - 1.378)^2}{2[18.75 - 6(5.772) + 9(1.378^2)]} = .771$$

> There is more than ample room for an error here, but if you calculate the individual bits one by one, and then lay them out clearly, you should have no problem getting the correct result.
>
> You can see here that the effective degrees of freedom are about 3/4 (.77) their original size.

14.9 Back to the calculator usage data in Exercise 14.6:

a. Plot

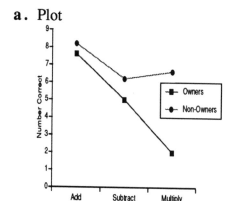

b. Analysis of simple effects:

Cell totals:	Problems			
	Add	Subt	Mult	Total
Owners	38	25	10	73
Non-Owners	41	31	33	105
Total	79	56	43	178

For the first three simple effects we're breaking down a combination of SS_{Groups} and SS_{PG} from the overall analysis in Exercise 14.6, so for the error term we will need to combine the error terms which were used to test MS_{Groups} and MS_{PG} in that analysis.

$$MS_{w/inCell} = \frac{MS_{Ss\ w/in\ grps} + MS_{P*Ss\ w/in\ grps}}{df_{Ss\ w/in\ grps} + df_{P*Ss\ w/in\ grps}} = \frac{33.066 + 10.934}{8 + 16} = 1.833$$

The df against which to evaluate F also must be adjusted for these simple effects. F_{obt} will be evaluated against $F'_{.05(g-1,f')}$ but we must first calculate f'.

$$f' = \frac{(u+v)^2}{\dfrac{u^2}{df_u} + \dfrac{v^2}{df_v}} = \frac{(33.066 + 10.934)^2}{\dfrac{33.066^2}{8} + \dfrac{10.934^2}{16}} = 13.431$$

$u = SS_{Ss\ w/in\ grps}$

$v = SS_{P*Ss\ w/in\ grps}$

With the error terms and degrees of freedom ready, we go ahead with calculating the sums of squares and testing them:

$$SS_{Grp\ at\ Add} = \frac{\Sigma T^2_{G\ at\ A}}{n} - \frac{T^2_A}{gn} = \frac{38^2 + 41^2}{5} - \frac{79^2}{2(5)} = 0.9$$

$$MS_{G\ at\ A} = \frac{SS_{G\ at\ A}}{df_{G\ at\ A}} = \frac{0.9}{1} = 0.9$$

$$F_{G\ at\ A} = \frac{MS_{G\ at\ A}}{MS_{w/in\ cell}} = \frac{0.9}{1.833} = <1$$

$$SS_{Grp\ at\ Subt} = \frac{\Sigma T^2_{G\ at\ S}}{n} - \frac{T^2_S}{gn} = \frac{25^2 + 31^2}{5} - \frac{56^2}{2(5)} = 3.6$$

$$MS_{G\ at\ S} = \frac{SS_{G\ at\ S}}{df_{G\ at\ S}} = \frac{3.6}{1} = 3.6$$

$$F_{G\ at\ S} = \frac{MS_{G\ at\ S}}{MS_{w/in\ cell}} = \frac{3.6}{1.833} = 1.96\ ns$$

$$SS_{\text{Grp at Mult}} = \frac{\Sigma T^2_{\text{G at M}}}{n} - \frac{T^2_M}{gn} = \frac{10^2 + 33^2}{5} - \frac{43^2}{2(5)} = 52.9$$

$$MS_{\text{G at M}} = \frac{SS_{\text{G at M}}}{df_{\text{G at M}}} = \frac{52.9}{1} = 52.9$$

$$F_{\text{G at M}} = \frac{MS_{\text{G at M}}}{MS_{\text{w/in cell}}} = \frac{52.9}{1.833} = 28.86^*$$

$*p < .05 \quad [F_{.05(g-1, f')} = F_{.05(1,13)} = 4.67]$

For the last two simple effects we're breaking down a combination of SS_{Problems} and SS_{PG} from the overall analysis in Exercise 14.6. Since MS_{Problems} and MS_{PG} were both tested by the same error term in that analysis ($MS_{\text{P*Ss w/in grps}}$) we could use that error term to test these simple effects. However, as pointed out in the chapter, violations of sphericity create serious problems when testing simple effects, and for that reason we will use separate error terms for the two analyses. The easiest way to do this is to run separate repeated measures analysis of variance for each group. This will produce the same sums of squares for the simple effect, as well as the appropriate error term.

The following results were produced by SPSS. Notice that the form of the printout is quite different from what we usually have. The order of terms is reversed, and the error term is given as "within+residual."

Calculator owners:

Source of Variation	SS	DF	MS	F	Sig of F
WITHIN+RESIDUAL	2.80	8	.35		
TASK	78.53	2	39.27	112.19	.000

- -

Non-owners

Source of Variation	SS	DF	MS	F	Sig of F
WITHIN+RESIDUAL	8.13	8	1.02		
TASK	11.20	2	5.60	5.51	.031

- -

The F is significant in both cases, indicating that Task made a difference. If we had used a pooled error term, MS_{error} would have been 0.683, which, because of the fact that the sample sizes were equal, is the average of the two error terms we used. But notice that the pooled error term would have been about 60% of what it was when we treat the groups separately.

14.11 From Exercise 14.10:

a. Simple effect of reading ability for children:

$$SS_{\text{Read at Child}} = \frac{\Sigma T^2_{R\text{ at }C}}{in} - \frac{T^2_C}{irn} = \frac{72^2 + 33^2}{3(5)} - \frac{105^2}{3(2)(5)} = 50.7$$

$$MS_{R\text{ at }C} = \frac{SS_{R\text{ at }C}}{df_{R\text{ at }C}} = \frac{50.7}{1} = 50.7$$

Because we are using only the data from Children, it would be wise not to use a pooled error term. The following is the relevant printout from SPSS for the Between-subject effect of Reader.

```
Tests of Between-Subjects Effects.

Tests of Significance for T1 using UNIQUE sums of squares
Source of Variation        SS      DF        MS        F  Sig of F

WITHIN+RESIDUAL          34.80       8      4.35
READ                    50.70       1     50.70     11.66      .009
```

b. Simple effect of items for adult good readers:

$$SS_{\text{Item at AG}} = \frac{\Sigma T^2_{I\text{ at }AG}}{n} - \frac{T^2_{AG}}{in} = \frac{31^2 + 30^2 + 25^2}{5} - \frac{86^2}{3(5)} = 4.133$$

Again, we do not want to pool error terms. The following is the relevant printout from SPSS for Adult Good readers. The difference is not significant, nor would it be for any decrease in the *df* if we used a correction factor.

```
Tests involving 'ITEMS' Within-Subject Effect.

AVERAGED Tests of Significance for MEAS.1 using UNIQUE sums of squares
Source of Variation        SS      DF        MS        F  Sig of F

WITHIN+RESIDUAL           4.53       8       .57
ITEMS                     4.13       2      2.07      3.65      .075
```

14.13 It would certainly affect the covariances because we would force a high level of covariance among items. As the number of responses classified at one level of Item went up, another item would have to go down.

> This result raises a general rule that is worth keeping in mind. It is usually a poor idea to impose a limit on responses such that the data are subject to an additional constraint. For example, when the sum of the responses for one subject must come out to 100%, or 25 points, or whatever, you are asking for trouble. In that case, given the first $t-1$ trials, I can easily compute what the last trial must be. You will see additional examples of this in Chapter 16.

14.15 Plot of results in Exercise 14.14:

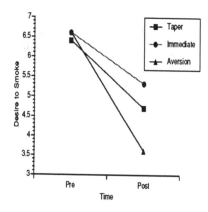

14.17 Analysis of data in Exercise 14.5 by BMDP:

a. Comparison with results obtained by hand in Exercise 14.5.

b. The F for Mean is a test on $H_0 : \mu = 0$.

c. $MS_{w/in\ Cell}$ is the average of the cell variances.

> But remember, $MS_{within\ Cell}$ contains both within and between subject variability. It is this between subject variability that we pull out to get a more refined error term for within subject effects.

14.19 Source column of summary table for 4-way ANOVA with repeated measures on A & B and independent measures on C & D.

Source
Between Ss
C
D
CD
Ss w/in groups
Within Ss
A
AC
AD

ACD
A x Ss w/in groups
B
BC
BD
BCD
B x Ss w/in groups
AB
ABC
ABD
ABCD
AB x Ss w/in groups
Total

14.21 Using Manova in Exercise 14.20 we have gained freedom from the sphericity assumption, but at the potential loss of a small amount of power.

> Although it is getting more common to see people run both univariate and multivariate analyses, the univariate analyses are still the most commonly reported. The problem with running both is in deciding what you are going to do if they disagree. You can't just take the result that you like best.

14.23 Analysis of Stress data:

Source	df	SS	MS	F	Pillai F	Prob
Between Subj	97	15.996				
Gender	1	7.296	7.296	5.64*		
Role	1	8.402	8.402	6.49*		
G * R	1	0.298	0.298	<1		
Ss w/in Grps	94	121.687	1.294			
Within Subj	97	87.390				
Time	1	1.064	1.064	1.23*	1.23	0.2700
T*G	1	0.451	0.451	<1	0.52	0.4720
T*R	1	0.001	0.001	<1	0.00	0.9708
T*G*R	1	4.652	4.652	5.38*	5.38	0.0225
T*Ss w/in grps	94	81.222	0.864			
Total	194	103.386				

*p < .05

The univariate and multivariate F values agree because we have only two levels of each independent variable.

14.25

a. You can create a new variable names NumTimes. This variable will be 1 when a person is present in only the first data set and 2 when they are present in both. You can then use NumTimes as a variable in the analysis of Time 1 data. When you do this, the F for NumTimes is 0.0002. Thus there is clearly no difference between the two groups in terms of our dependent variable. All of the interactions of NumTimes with the other variables are also nonsignificant.

b. If there had been differences due to this variable, I would be concerned that there might be systematic differences in the subjects who enter the study late or who drop out, and thus my results might not apply to a general population.

It is now becoming common for reviewers and editors to ask for this kind of an analysis when there are more than a few missing observation. You should be prepared to perform analyses like this, and should in fact do it without being asked.

Chapter 15 - Multiple Regression

15.1 Predicting Quality of Life:

a. All other variables held constant, a difference of +1 degree in Temperature is associated with a difference of −.01 in perceived Quality of Life. A difference of $1000 in median Income, again all other variables held constant, is associated with a +.05 difference in perceived Quality of Life. A similar interpretation applies to b_3 and b_4. Since values of 0.00 cannot reasonably occur for all predictors, the intercept has no meaningful interpretation.

b. $\hat{Y} = 5.37 - .01(55) + .05(12) + .003(500) - .01(200) = 4.92$

c. $\hat{Y} = 5.37 - .01(55) + .05(12) + .003(100) - .01(200) = 3.72$

> Equations like this occur quite often, and are often misinterpreted. Keep in mind that the phrase "all other things held constant" always applies. That's what often gets left out in newspaper accounts.

15.3 The F values for the four regression coefficients would be as follows:

$$F_1 = \left[\frac{\beta_1}{s_{\beta_1}}\right]^2 = \left[\frac{-0.438}{0.397}\right]^2 = 1.22 \qquad F_2 = \left[\frac{\beta_2}{s_{\beta_2}}\right]^2 = \left[\frac{0.762}{0.252}\right]^2 = 9.14$$

$$F_3 = \left[\frac{\beta_3}{s_{\beta_3}}\right]^2 = \left[\frac{0.081}{0.052}\right]^2 = 2.43 \qquad F_4 = \left[\frac{\beta_4}{s_{\beta_4}}\right]^2 = \left[\frac{-0.132}{0.025}\right]^2 = 27.88$$

I would thus delete Temperature, since it has the smallest F, and therefore the smallest semi-partial correlation with the dependent variable.

> Remember the little sentence in the text that says that a t or an F test on b or β will order the variables in exactly the same way they would be ordered by the squared semi-partial correlation.

15.5 **a.** Envir has the largest semi-partial correlation with the criterion, because it has the largest value of t.

b. The gain in prediction (from $r = .58$ to $R = .697$) which we obtain by using all the predictors is more than offset by the loss of power we sustain as p became large relative to N.

15.7 As the correlation between two variables decreases, the amount of variance in a third variable that they share decreases. Thus the higher will be the possible squared semi-partial correlation of each variable with the criterion. They each can account for more previously unexplained variation.

> It may help to understand the answer to this question if you go back to the Venn diagrams. Notice that when variables are independent, the circles do not overlap. As the correlation between variables increases, so does the overlap of their circles. And as the circles overlap more, they cover less of the total variation of the criterion.

15.9 The tolerance column shows us that NumSup and Respon are fairly well correlated with the other predictors, whereas Yrs is nearly independent of them.

> Remember that the tolerance is the correlation of one *predictor* with all other *predictors*. (The criterion doesn't play any role in the tolerance.)

15.11 Using Y and $\hat{Y}$ from Exercise 15.10:

$$MS_{residual} = \frac{\Sigma(Y - \hat{Y})^2}{(N - p - 1)}$$

$$= \frac{42.322}{15 - 4 - 1} = 4.232 \quad \text{[as also calculated by BMDP in Exercise 15.4]}$$

15.13 Adjusted R^2 for 15 cases in Exercise 15.9:

$$R^2_{0.1234} = .173$$

$$\text{est } R^{*2} = 1 - \frac{(1 - R^2)(N - 1)}{(N - p - 1)} = 1 - \frac{(1 - .173)(14)}{(15 - 4 - 1)} = -.158$$

Since a squared value cannot be negative, we will declare it undefined. This is all the more reasonable in light of the fact that we cannot reject $H_0\, \mathcal{R}^* = 0$.

> This is a nice example of how what looks like a decent, though low, correlation when you have lots of predictors in relationship to the number of observations, can turn out to be misleading. If you have a small sample size, try to use very few predictors. And don't use a lot of predictors even if you have huge sample sizes—it rarely does any good.

15.15 Using the first three variables from Exercise 15.4:

    a. Figure comparable to Figure 15.1:

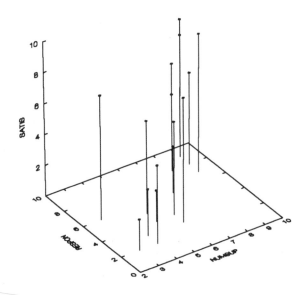

    b. $\hat{Y} = .4067\text{Respon} + .1845\text{NumSup} + 2.3542$

The slope of the plane with respect to the Respon axis $(X_1) = .4067$
The slope of the plane with respect to the NumSup axis $(X_2) = .1845$
The plane intersects the Y axis at 2.3542

> Isn't that a neat plot!? I plotted it with Systat, but most computer software (especially for microcomputers) will do this for you.

15.17 It has no meaning in that we have the data for the population of interest (the 10 districts).

> Well, perhaps that's a bit abrupt. What I'm getting at is that the multiple correlation coefficient that we calculate here will be exactly equal to R*, because we are calculating the correlation on the whole population. But that doesn't mean that we don't care whether the population correlation is .08 or .92. We certainly do care about that.

15.19 It plays a major role through its correlation with the residual components of the other variables.

15.21 Within the context of a multiple-regression equation, we cannot look at one variable alone. The slope for one variable is only the slope for that variable when all other variables are held constant. The percentage of mothers not seeking care until the third trimester is correlated with a number of other variables.

It is important to remember that correlation and causation are different things. What may look like a causal relationship may be something else entirely. At the same time, it is certainly worth knowing whether there is a relationship (causal or otherwise) between two variables.

15.23 Computer exercise examining residuals.

15.25 Rerun of Exercise 15.24 adding PVTotal.

Adding PVTotal to the model does not improve the fit. R^2 increased by only .0001 and the standard error actually went up. The standard error for PVLoss jumped dramatically, from .1049 to .1777. This can be attributed to the fact that PVTotal was highly correlated with PVLoss.

First of all, don't throw in the kitchen sink just to see if it will fit. And when you do add variables, look for variables that are not substantially correlated with the predictors you are already using.

15.27 Path diagram showing the relationships among the variables in the model.

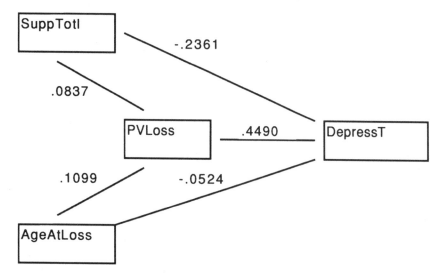

Path diagrams are very popular in the social sciences. There are much more sophisticated ways of creating such models that better deal with the error in your variables, but the approach used here is simple and intuitively meaningful.

15.29 Regression diagnostics.

Case # 104 has the largest value of Cook's D (.137) but not a very large Studentized residual ($t = -1.88$). When we delete this case the squared multiple correlation is increased slightly. More importantly, the standard error of regression and the standard error of one of the predictors (PVLoss) also decrease slightly. This case is not sufficiently extreme to have a major impact on the data.

15.31 Logistic regression using Harass.dat:

The dependent variable (Reporting) is the last variable in the data set.

I cannot provide all possible models, so I am including just the most complete. This is a less than optimal model, but it provides a good starting point. This result was given by SPSS.

```
Variable(s) Entered on Step Number
1..       AGE
          MARSTAT   Marital Status
          FEMIDEOL
          FREQUENC  Frequency of behavior
          OFFENS    Offensiveness

Estimation terminated at iteration number 3 because
Log Likelihood decreased by less than .01 percent.

   -2 Log Likelihood        439.984
   Goodness of Fit          338.971

                      Chi-Square    df Significance

   Model Chi-Square      35.442      5     .0000
   Improvement           35.442      5     .0000

Classification Table for REPORT
                  Predicted
               No      Yes      Percent Correct
               N       Y

Observed
   No    N     111      63       63.79%

   Yes   Y      77      92       54.44%

                      Overall   59.18%

-------------------- Variables in the Equation --------------------

Variable       B        S.E.     Wald     df    Sig      R      Exp(B)

AGE          -.0137    .0129   1.1264     1   .2886   .0000    .9864
MARSTAT      -.0723    .2339    .0954     1   .7574   .0000    .9303
FEMIDEOL      .0070    .0146    .2275     1   .6334   .0000   1.0070
FREQUENC     -.0464    .1526    .0925     1   .7610   .0000    .9547
OFFENS        .4878    .0949  26.4310     1   .0000   .2267   1.6287
Constant    -1.7317   1.4298   1.4670     1   .2258
```

From this set of predictors we see that overall $\chi^2_{LR} = 35.44$, which is significant on 5 *df* with a *p* value of .0000 (to 4 decimal places). The only predictor that contributes significantly is the Offensiveness of the behavior, which has a Wald χ^2 of 26.43. The exponentiation of the regression coefficient yields 0.9547. This would suggest that as the offensiveness of the behavior increases, the likelihood of reporting *decreases*. That's an odd result. But remember that we have all variables in the model. If we simply predicting reporting by using Offensiveness, exp(B) = 1.65, which means that a 1 point increase in

Offensiveness multiplies the odds of reporting by 1.65. Obviously we have some work to do to make sense of these data. I leave that to you.

> This is obviously not the strongest logistic model you are ever likely to see, but it illustrates some important points. Be sure that you understand how logistic regression relates to standard multiple linear regression. Do not expect to run a logistic regression by hand, even if you have nothing better to do.

15.33 It may well be that the frequency of the behavior is tied in with its offensiveness, which is related to the likelihood of reporting. In fact, the correlation between those two variables is .20, which is significant at $p < .000$. (I think my explanation would be more convincing if Frequency were a significant predictor when used on its own.)

> The correlations among the predictor variables can make it very difficult sometimes to interpret a result. Just keep in mind that what may seem like a clear variable to you may, in reality, be quite a different thing in the real world.

15.37 This should cause them to pause. It is impossible to change one of the variables without changing the interaction variable in which that variable plays a role. In other words, I can't think of a sensible interpretation of "holding all other variables constant" in this situation.

> Although it is difficult to think of a sensible interpretation of "holding all other things constant" when one variable is created from another, interactive relationships are very important in psychology. Don't throw out the baby with the bath water and assume that they are too difficult to use.

Chapter 16 - Analysis of Variance and Covariance as General Linear Models

16.1 Eye fixations per line of text for poor, average, and good readers:

a. Design matrix, using only the first subject in each group:

$$X = \begin{bmatrix} 1 & 0 \\ 0 & 1 \\ -1 & -1 \end{bmatrix}$$

> Notice that there is one column per degree of freedom, and that the last group is coded -1 in both columns.

b. Computer exercise:

$$R^2 = .608 \quad SS_{reg} = 57.7333 \quad SS_{residual} = 37.2000$$

c. Analysis of variance:

$T_1 = 41$

$T_2 = 28$

$$SS_{total} = \Sigma X^2 - \frac{(\Sigma X)^2}{N} = 588 - \frac{86^2}{15} = 94.933$$

$T_3 = 17$

$$SS_{group} = \frac{\Sigma T_j^2}{n} - \frac{(\Sigma X)^2}{N} = \frac{41^2 + 28^2 + 17^2}{5} - \frac{86^2}{15} = 57.733$$

$\Sigma X = 86$

$N = 15$

$$SS_{error} = SS_{total} - SS_{group} = 94.933 - 57.733 = 37.200$$

$n = 5$

Source	df	SS	MS	F
Group	2	57.733	28.867	9.312*
Error	12	37.200	3.100	
Total	14	94.933		

$*p < .05 \quad [F_{.05(2,12)} = 3.89]$

> Notice that SS_{group} and SS_{error} are the same as SS_{reg} and $SS_{residual}$.

16.3 Data from Exercise 16.1, modified to make unequal ns:

$$R^2 = .624 \quad SS_{reg} = 79.0095 \quad SS_{residual} = 47.6571$$

Analysis of variance:

$$T_1 = 41 \qquad n_1 = 5$$
$$T_2 = 41 \qquad n_2 = 7$$
$$T_3 = 30 \qquad n_3 = 9$$

$$\Sigma X = 112$$
$$N = 21$$

$$SS_{total} = \Sigma X^2 - \frac{(\Sigma X)^2}{N} = 724 - \frac{112^2}{21} = 126.6666$$

$$SS_{group} = \frac{\Sigma T_j^2}{n} - \frac{(\Sigma X)^2}{N} = \frac{41^2}{5} + \frac{41^2}{7} + \frac{30^2}{9} - \frac{112^2}{21} = 79.0095$$

$$SS_{error} = SS_{total} - SS_{group} = 126.6666 - 79.0095 = 47.6571$$

Source	df	SS	MS	F
Group	2	79.0095	39.5048	14.92*
Error	18	47.6571	2.6476	
Total	20	126.6666		

$*p < .05 \quad [F_{.05(2,18)} = 3.55]$

16.5 Relationship between Gender, SES, and Locus of Control:

a. Analysis of Variance:

		SES				
		Low	Avg	High		
Gender	Male	98	114	138	350	
	Female	66	98	130	294	
		164	212	268	644 = ΣX	

$$\Sigma X^2 = 9418$$
$$N = 48$$
$$n = 8$$
$$g = 2$$
$$s = 3$$

$$SS_{total} = \Sigma X^2 - \frac{(\Sigma X)^2}{N} = 9418 - \frac{644^2}{48} = 777.6667$$

$$SS_G = \frac{\Sigma T_G^2}{sn} - \frac{(\Sigma X)^2}{N} \qquad\qquad SS_S = \frac{\Sigma T_S^2}{gn} - \frac{(\Sigma X)^2}{N}$$

$$= \frac{350^2 + 294^2}{3(8)} - \frac{644^2}{48} \qquad\qquad = \frac{164^2 + 212^2 + 268^2}{2(8)} - \frac{644^2}{48}$$

$$= 65.3333 \qquad\qquad\qquad\qquad = 338.6667$$

$$SS_{GS} = SS_{cells} - SS_G - SS_S = 422.6667 - 65.3333 - 338.6667 = 18.6667$$

$$SS_{error} = SS_{total} - SS_{cells} = 777.6667 - 422.6667 = 355.0000$$

Source	df	SS	MS	F
Gender	1	65.333	65.333	7.730*
SES	2	338.667	169.333	20.034*
G x S	2	18.667	9.333	1.104
Error	42	355.000	8.452	
Total	47	777.667		

$*p < .05 \quad [F_{.05(1,42)} = 4.08; F_{.05(2,42)} = 3.23]$

b. ANOVA summary table constructed from sums of squares calculated from design matrix:

$$SS_G = SS_{reg(\alpha,\beta,\alpha\beta)} - SS_{reg(\beta,\alpha\beta)} = 422.6667 - 357.3333 = 65.333$$

$$SS_S = SS_{reg(\alpha,\beta,\alpha\beta)} - SS_{reg(\alpha,\alpha\beta)} = 422.6667 - 84.0000 = 338.667$$

$$SS_{GS} = SS_{reg(\alpha,\beta,\alpha\beta)} - SS_{reg(\alpha,\beta)} = 422.6667 - 404.000 = 18.667$$

$$SS_{total} = SS_Y = 777.667$$

The summary table is exactly the same as in part a (above).

The two sets of sums of squares should always be the same with equal sample sizes, and will generally be the same with unequal sample sizes so long as the statistical software calculates the appropriate sums of squares. With SAS, this means Type III SS, and with SPSS this means Unique SS. (BMDP will always produce these sums of squares.)

16.7 The data from Exercise 16.5 modified to make unequal *n*s:

$$SS_{error} = SS_Y - SS_{reg(\alpha,\beta,\alpha\beta)} = 750.1951 - 458.7285 = 291.467$$

$$SS_G = SS_{reg(\alpha,\beta,\alpha\beta)} - SS_{reg(\beta,\alpha\beta)} = 458.7285 - 398.7135 = 60.015$$

$$SS_S = SS_{reg(\alpha,\beta,\alpha\beta)} - SS_{reg(\alpha,\alpha\beta)} = 458.7285 - 112.3392 = 346.389$$

$$SS_{GS} = SS_{reg(\alpha,\beta,\alpha\beta)} - SS_{reg(\alpha,\beta)} = 458.7285 - 437.6338 = 21.095$$

Source	df	SS	MS	F
Gender	1	60.015	60.015	7.21*
SES	2	346.389	173.195	20.80*
G x S	2	21.095	10.547	1.27
Error	35	291.467	8.328	
Total	40			

$*p < .05 \quad [F_{.05(1,35)} = 4.12; F_{.05(2,35)} = 3.27]$

> This analysis in Exercise 16.7 will always give the same results as those referred to in the note to Exercise 16.5, even with unequal sample sizes.

16.9 Model from data in Exercise 16.5:

$$1.1667A_1 - 3.1667B_1 - 0.1667B_2 + 0.8333AB_{11} - 0.1667AB_{12} + 13.4167$$

Means:

		SES (B)			
		Low	Avg	High	
Gender (A)	Male	12.25	14.25	17.25	14.583
	Female	8.25	12.25	16.25	12.250
		10.25	13.25	16.75	$13.4167 = \overline{X}..$

$$\hat{\mu} = \overline{X}.. = 13.4167 = b_0 = \text{intercept}$$

$$\hat{\alpha}_1 = \overline{A}_1 - \overline{X}.. = 14.583 - 13.4167 = 1.1667 = b_1$$

$$\hat{\beta}_1 = \overline{B}_1 - \overline{X}.. = 10.25 - 13.4167 = -3.1667 = b_2$$

$$\hat{\beta}_2 = \overline{B}_2 - \overline{X}.. = 13.25 - 13.4167 = -0.1667 = b_3$$

$$\hat{\alpha\beta}_{11} = \overline{AB}_{11} - \overline{A}_1 - \overline{B}_1 + \overline{X}.. = 12.25 - 14.583 - 10.25 + 13.4167 = 0.8337 = b_4$$

$$\hat{\alpha\beta}_{12} = \overline{AB}_{12} - \overline{A}_1 - \overline{B}_2 + \overline{X}.. = 14.25 - 14.583 - 13.250 + 13.4167 = -0.1667 = b_5$$

> This approach will produce the correct treatment effects, regardless of whether or not we have equal sample sizes.

16.11 Does Method I really deal with unweighted means?

Means:

	B_1	B_2	weighted	unweighted
A_1	4	10	8.5	7
B_2	10	4	8	7
weighted	8	8.5	8.29	
unweighted	7	7		7

The full model produced by Method 1: $\hat{Y} = 0.0A_1 + 0.0B_1 - 3.0AB_{11} + 7.0$

Effects calculated on weighted means:

$$\hat{\mu} = \overline{X}.. = 8.29 \neq b_0 = \text{intercept}$$

$$\hat{\alpha}_1 = \overline{A}_1 - \overline{X}.. = 8.5 - 8.29 = .21 \neq b_1$$

$$\hat{\beta}_1 = \overline{B}_1 - \overline{X}.. = 8.0 - 8.29 = -.29 \neq b_2$$

$$\hat{\alpha\beta}_{11} = \overline{AB}_{11} - \overline{A}_1 - \overline{B}_1 + \overline{X}.. = 4.00 - 8.5 + 8.29 = -4.21 \neq b_3$$

Effects calculated on unweighted means:

$$\hat{\mu} = \overline{X}.. = 7.00 = b_0 = \text{intercept}$$

$$\hat{\alpha}_1 = \overline{A}_1 - \overline{X}.. = 7.0 - 7.0 = 0.0 = b_1$$

$$\hat{\beta}_1 = \overline{B}_1 - \overline{X}.. = 7.0 - 7.0 = 0.0 = b_2$$

$$\hat{\alpha\beta}_{11} = \overline{AB}_{11} - \overline{A}_1 - \overline{B}_1 + \overline{X}.. = 4.0 - 7.0 - 7.0 + 7.0 = -3 = b_3$$

These coefficients found by the model clearly reflect the effects computed on unweighted means. Alternately, carrying out the complete analysis leads to $SS_A = SS_B = 0.00$, again reflecting equality of unweighted means.

> The fact that this works with unequal sample sizes means that it will also work with equal sample sizes.
>
> Because the treatment effects for an independent variable sum to 0, you can calculate the missing ones by subtraction. Since the estimate of β_1 is 0, the estimate of β_2 would also be 0. Because $\alpha\beta_{11}$ is –3, the $\alpha\beta_{12}$ must be +3. The same for $\alpha\beta_{21}$, since this is only a 2x2 design.

16.13 Venn diagram representing the sums of squares in Exercise 16.7:

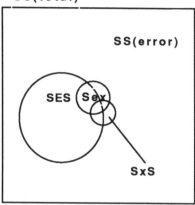

SS(total)

SS(error)

SES **Sex**

SxS

> It is important to note that the degree of overlap among the circles comes from the unequal sample sizes. It has nothing to do with the values of the dependent variable, only with the degree of inequality of the n_i.

16.15 Energy consumption of families:

a. Design matrix, using only the first entry in each group for illustration purposes:

$$X = \begin{bmatrix} 1 & 0 & 58 & 75 \\ \cdots & \cdots & \cdots & \cdots \\ 0 & 1 & 60 & 70 \\ \cdots & \cdots & \cdots & \cdots \\ -1 & -1 & 75 & 80 \end{bmatrix}$$

b. Analysis of covariance:

$$SS_{reg(\alpha, cov, \alpha c)} = 2424.6202$$

$$SS_{reg(\alpha, cov)} = 2369.2112$$

$$SS_{residual} = 246.5221 = SS_{error}$$

There is not a significant decrement in SS_{reg} and thus we can continue to assume homogeneity of regression.

$$SS_{reg(\alpha)} = 1118.5333$$

$$SS_{cov} = SS_{reg(\alpha,cov)} - SS_{reg(\alpha)} = 2369.2112 - 1118.5333 = 1250.6779$$

$$SS_{reg(cov)} = 1716.2884$$

$$SS_A = SS_{reg(\alpha,cov)} - SS_{reg(cov)} = 2369.2112 - 1716.2884 = 652.9228$$

Source	df	SS	MS	F
Covariate	1	1250.6779	1250.6779	55.81*
A (Group)	2	652.9228	326.4614	14.57*
Error	11	246.5221	22.4111	
Total	14	2615.7333		

$*p < .05 \quad [F_{.05(1,11)} = 4.84; F_{.05(2,11)} = 3.98]$

> It is important to note that the analysis of covariance in very much like the analysis of variance. The covariate is just another variable, although we hope that it does not interact with the independent variables.

16.17 Adjusted means for the data in Exercise 16.16:

(The order of the means may differ depending on how you code the group membership and how the software sets up its design matrix. But the numerical values should agree.)

$$\hat{Y} = -7.9099A_1 + 0.8786A_2 - 2.4022B + 0.5667AB_{11} + 0.1311AB_{21} + 0.7260C + 6.3740$$

$$\begin{aligned}
\hat{Y}_{11} = &-7.9099(1) + 0.8786(0) - 2.4022(1) + 0.5667(1) + 0.1311(0) \\
&+ 0.7260(61.3333) + 6.3740 = 41.1566
\end{aligned}$$

$$\begin{aligned}
\hat{Y}_{12} = &-7.9099(1) + 0.8786(0) - 2.4022(-1) + 0.5667(-1) + 0.1311(0) \\
&+ 0.7260(61.3333) + 6.3740 = 44.8276
\end{aligned}$$

$$\begin{aligned}
\hat{Y}_{21} = &-7.9099(0) + 0.8786(1) - 2.4022(1) + 0.5667(0) + 0.1311(1) \\
&+ 0.7260(61.3333) + 6.3740 = 49.5095
\end{aligned}$$

$$\begin{aligned}
\hat{Y}_{22} = &-7.9099(0) + 0.8786(1) - 2.4022(-1) + 0.5667(0) + 0.1311(-1) \\
&+ 0.7260(61.3333) + 6.3740 = 54.0517
\end{aligned}$$

$$\begin{aligned}
\hat{Y}_{31} = &-7.9099(-1) + 0.8786(-1) - 2.4022(1) + 0.5667(-1) + 0.1311(-1) \\
&+ 0.7260(61.3333) + 6.3740 = 54.8333
\end{aligned}$$

$$\hat{Y}_{32} = -7.9099(-1) + 0.8786(-1) - 2.4022(-1) + 0.5667(1) + 0.1311(1)$$
$$+ 0.7260(61.3333) + 6.3740 = 61.0333$$

> The covariate is always given the value of 61.3333 in this problem because we want to evaluate the dependent variable *as if* the different cells of the design all had the same value of the covariate mean, which is 61.3333.

16.19 Computer exercise.

16.23 Analysis of variance on the covariate from Exercise 16.22.

The following is abbreviated SAS output.

General Linear Models Procedure

Dependent Variable: YEARCOLL

Source	DF	Squares	Square	F Value	Pr > F
Model	5	13.3477645	2.6695529	2.15	0.0600
Error	292	363.0012288	1.2431549		
Corrected Total	297	376.3489933			

	R-Square	C.V.	Root MSE	YEARCOLL Mean
	0.035466	41.53258	1.11497	2.6845638

Source	DF	Type III SS	Mean Square	F Value	Pr > F
GENDER	1	5.95006299	5.95006299	4.79	0.0295
GROUP	2	0.78070431	0.39035216	0.31	0.7308
GENDER*GROUP	2	2.96272310	1.4813615519	0.3052	

GENDER	GROUP	YEARCOLL LSMEAN
1	1	2.27906977
1	2	2.53225806
1	3	2.68421053
2	1	2.88888889
2	2	2.85000000
2	3	2.70967742

These data reveal a significant difference between males and females in terms of YearColl. Females are slightly ahead of males. If the first year of college is in fact more stressful than later years, this could account for some of the difference we found in Exercise 16.21.

> It is a good idea to run an analysis of variance on the covariate itself whenever you are interested in an analysis of covariance. It will tell you much about your assumptions and about what is happening with the covariate.

16.25 A slope of 1.0 would mean that the treatment added a constant to people's pretest scores, which seems somewhat unlikely. Students might try taking any of the data in the book with a pretest and posttest score and plotting the relationship.

> This relationship between the analysis of covariance and difference scores suggests that it is usually preferable to run an analysis of covariance in this situation unless you have a particular interest in the difference scores.

Chapter 17 - Log-Linear Models

17.1 Possible models for data on idiomatic communication.

$$\ln(F_{ij}) = \lambda \qquad\qquad \text{Equiprobability}$$

$$\ln(F_{ij}) = \lambda + \lambda^F \qquad\qquad \text{Conditional equiprobability on Function}$$

$$\ln(F_{ij}) = \lambda + \lambda^I \qquad\qquad \text{Conditional equiprobability on Inventor}$$

$$\ln(F_{ij}) = \lambda + \lambda^F + \lambda^I \qquad\qquad \text{Independence}$$

$$\ln(F_{ij}) = \lambda + \lambda^F + \lambda^I + \lambda^{FI} \qquad\qquad \text{Saturated model}$$

> In this situation we probably would have no real interest in the first three models—they seem very unlikely. We really want to compare the Independence model against the Saturated model, usually hoping that the Independence model is not a good fit, requiring us to conclude that there is an interaction between the variables.

17.3 Lambda values for the complete (saturated) model.

a. $\lambda = 2.8761 = \text{mean of } \ln(\text{cell}_{ij})$

b. $\lambda^{\text{Inventor}} = .199\ .540\ -.739$

The effect for "female partner" is .199, indicating that the ln(frequencies in row 1) are slightly above average.

c. $\lambda^{\text{Function}} = -.632\ .260\ .222\ -.007\ .097\ -.667\ .303\ -.029\ .452$

The effect of Confrontation in -.632. Confrontation contributes somewhat less than its share of idiosyncratic expressions.

4) $\lambda^{\text{Inventor * Function}} = $

$$\begin{array}{ccccc} .196 & -.039 & \ldots & .249 & .028 \\ -.481 & .038 & \ldots & .250 & .259 \\ .286 & .001 & \ldots & -.500 & -.287 \end{array}$$

The unique effect of cell$_{11}$ is .196. It contributes slightly more than would be predicted from the row and column totals above.

> Remember that λ in log-linear models plays a role analogous to the treatment effects (α or β) in the analysis of variance.

17.5 For females the odds in favor of a direct hit are 6.00, whereas for males they are only 2.8125. This leaves an odds ratio of 6.00/2.8125 = 2.1333. A female is 2.1333 times more likely to have a direct hit than a male.

17.7 Letting S represent Satisfaction, G represent Gender, and V represent Validity, and with 0.50 added to all cells because of small frequencies, the optimal model is

$$\ln(Fij) = \lambda + \lambda^G + \lambda^S + \lambda^V + \lambda^{SV}$$

For this model $\chi^2 = 4.53$ on 5 *df*; $p = .4763$

An appropriate model for these data must take into account differences due to Satisfaction, Gender, and Validity. It must also take into account differences associated with a Satisfaction X Validity interaction. However, there are not relationships involving any of the other interactions.

> The fact that Gender must be a part of the model simply reflects the fact that there more more females than males in this study. It doesn't speak to the issue of whether females were more or less satisfied, etc. That is an important point to keep in mind.

17.9 Compare statistics from alternative designs:

You should examine the pattern of changes in the alternative designs. Although the marginal frequencies stay constant from design to design, the chi-square tests on those effects, the values of λ, and the tests on λ change as variables are added. This differs from what we see in the analysis of variance, where sums of squares remain unchanged as we look at additional independent variables (all other things equal).

> Here, again, we come across the fundamental difference between an analysis of variance and log-linear models. I may be overplaying this difference, but failure to recognize it leads people into trouble. You think you know what you are talking about and all of a sudden you don't.

17.11 Odds of being classed as adult delinquent.

Odds delinquent:
    Normal Testosterone, Low SES = 190/1104 = .1721
    High Testosterone, Low SES   = 62/140 = .4429
    Normal Testosterone, High SES = 53/1114 = .0476
    High Testosterone, High SES   =   3/70 = .0429

> Notice how these odds differ from one condition to another, telling us that there really is something meaningful in our data. The calculation of odds ratios in the next exercise makes this even clearer.

17.13 Optimal model for Dabbs and Morris (1990) Testosterone data.

The following is an SPSS program and the resulting output. The optimal model that results is one including all main effects and first order interactions, but not the three-way interactions. The value of χ^2 for this model is 3.52 on 1 df, for p = .0607. If any main effect or interaction were dropped from the model, the χ^2 would be significant. The parameter estimates are based on the saturated model—the standard SPSS approach.

```
TITLE  'SPSS loglinear analysis on Testosterone Data'
Set Width=80
FILE HANDLE DATA /NAME = '[d_howell.book]Testost.dat'
DATA LIST FILE = DATA  Free
                    / SES Delinq Testost Freq
Weight by Freq
Value labels   SES 1 'Low' 2 'High'/
               Delinq 1 'Yes' 2 'No'/
               Testost 1 'Normal' 2 'High'/
Hiloglinear    SES (1,2)Delinq (1,2) Testost (1,2)/
               Print Estim, Association/
               Design=SES*Delinq*Testost/
               Design=SES*Delinq SES*Testost Delinq*Testost/
```

Note: For saturated models 0.500 has been added to all observed cells.
- -
Goodness-of-fit test statistics

Likelihood ratio chi square =   .00000 DF = 0 P = 1.000
          Pearson chi square =   .00000 DF = 0 P = 1.000

- -

Tests that K-way and higher order effects are zero.

K	DF	L.R. Chisq	Prob	Pearson Chisq	Prob	Iteration
3	1	3.518	.0607	2.988	.0839	3
2	4	185.825	.0000	218.034	.0000	2
1	7	4085.232	.0000	4653.105	.0000	0

- -

Tests that K-way effects are zero.

K	DF	L.R. Chisq	Prob	Pearson Chisq	Prob	Iteration
1	3	3899.407	.0000	4435.071	.0000	0
2	3	182.307	.0000	215.046	.0000	0
3	1	3.518	.0607	2.988	.0839	0

Effect Name	DF	Partial Chisq	Prob	Iter
SES*DELINQ	1	98.559	.0000	2
SES*TESTOST	1	31.678	.0000	2
DELINQ*TESTOST	1	24.380	.0000	2
SES	1	23.988	.0000	2
DELINQ	1	1867.516	.0000	2
TESTOST	1	2007.903	.0000	2

- -

Estimates for Parameters.

SES*DELINQ*TESTOST

Parameter	Coeff.	Std. Err.	Z-Value	Lower 95 CI	Upper 95 CI
1	-.1142281423	.07382	-1.54739	-.25892	.03046

SES*DELINQ

Parameter	Coeff.	Std. Err.	Z-Value	Lower 95 CI	Upper 95 CI
1	.4339740600	.07382	5.87883	.28929	.57866

SES*TESTOST

Parameter	Coeff.	Std. Err.	Z-Value	Lower 95 CI	Upper 95 CI
1	-.2888801196	.07382	-3.91331	-.43357	-.14419

DELINQ*TESTOST

Parameter	Coeff.	Std. Err.	Z-Value	Lower 95 CI	Upper 95 CI
1	-.1226355817	.07382	-1.66128	-.26732	.02205

SES

Parameter	Coeff.	Std. Err.	Z-Value	Lower 95 CI	Upper 95 CI
1	.6041194722	.07382	8.18370	.45943	.74881

DELINQ

Parameter	Coeff.	Std. Err.	Z-Value	Lower 95 CI	Upper 95 CI
1	-1.075858250	.07382	-14.57410	-1.22055	-.93117

TESTOST

Parameter	Coeff.	Std. Err.	Z-Value	Lower 95 CI	Upper 95 CI
1	1.0829866625	.0738	14.67067	.93830	1.22767

- -

* * * * * H I E R A R C H I C A L   L O G   L I N E A R * * * *

DESIGN 2 has generating class
     SES*DELINQ
     SES*TESTOST
     DELINQ*TESTOST
- -
Goodness-of-fit test statistics
          Likelihood ratio chi square =   3.51824 DF = 1 P =   .061
                 Pearson chi square =   2.98809 DF = 1 P =   .084
- -

17.15 The complete solution for Pugh's (1984) data would take pages to present. Pugh selected the model that includes Fault*Verdict and Gender*Moral*verdict. This model has a $\chi^2 = 6.71$ on 10 df, with an associated probability of .7529. This is the model that BMDP4F would select if you chose a significance level of .15 for your cutoff.

Pugh (1984) derived her potential solutions from a theoretical analysis of the hypotheses. She tested the following models and obtained the accompanying χ^2 statistics. It would be instructive for students to compare these theoretically tested models against standard approaches to model building.

Model	Test of Fit			Added Effect Difference		
	df	χ^2	p	df	χ^2	p
GM,F,V	16	70.98	<.001			
GM,GF,V	15	70.93	<.001	1	.05	>.05
GM,GF,MF,V	13	68.06	<.001	2	2.87	>.05
GM,GF,MF,FV	12	32.68	<.01	1	35.38	<.001
GM,GF,MF,FV,GV	11	23.16	<.02	1	9.52	<.01
GM,GF,MF,FV,GV,MV	9	15.07	>.05	2	8.09	<.02
GM,MF,FV,GMV	7	3.71	>.05	2	11.36	<.01
GMV,GMF,GFV,MFV	2	2.94	>.05	5	0.77	>.05
FV,GMV	10	6.71	>.05	3	3.00	>.05

Chapter 18 - Nonparametric and Distribution-Free Statistical Tests

18.1 Inferences in children's story summaries (McConaughy, 1980):

a. Analysis using Wilcoxon's rank-sum test:

	Younger Children								Older Children					
Raw Data:	0	1	0	3	2	5	2		4	7	6	4	8	7
Ranks:	1.5	3	1.5	6	4.5	9	4.5		7.5	11.5	10	7.5	13	11.5

$\Sigma R = 30 \qquad N = 7 \qquad\qquad \Sigma R = 61 \qquad N = 6$

$W_s = \Sigma R$ for group with smaller $N = 61 \qquad W_s' = 2\overline{W} - W_s = 84 - 61 = 23$

$W_s' < W_s$, therefore use W_s' in Appendix W_s'. Double the probability level for a 2-tailed test.

$W_{.025(6,7)} = 27 > 23$

b. Reject H_0 and conclude that older children include more inferences in their summaries.

> We use Wilcoxon's Rank-Sum test here because we have different subjects in each of two groups. You know that they are different subjects because they differ in age. Thus, unless this was a longitudinal study that looked at children as they grew older, these must be independent groups of children.

18.3 The analysis in Exercise 18.2 using the normal approximation:

$$z = \frac{W_s - \dfrac{n_1(n_1 + n_2 + 1)}{2}}{\sqrt{\dfrac{n_1 n_2 (n_1 + n_2 + 1)}{12}}} = \frac{53 - \dfrac{9(9 + 11 + 1)}{2}}{\sqrt{\dfrac{9(11)(9 + 11 + 1)}{12}}} = -3.15$$

z	p
3.00	.0013
3.15	.0009
3.25	.0006

$p(z> = \pm 3.15) = 2(.0009) = .0018 < .05$

Reject H_0, which was the same conclusion as we came to in Exercise 18.2.

> Again, we use the Rank-Sum test because we have different groups of subjects.

120

18.5 Hypothesis formation in psychiatric residents (Nurcombe & Fitzhenry-Coor, 1979):

a. Analysis using Wilcoxon's matched-pairs signed-ranks test:

Before:	8	4	2	2	4	8	3	1	3	9
After:	7	9	3	6	3	10	6	7	8	7
Difference:	-1	+5	+1	+4	-1	+2	+3	+6	+5	-2
Rank:	2	8.5	2	7	2	4.5	6	10	8.5	4.5
Signed		8.5	2	7		4.5	6	10	8.5	
Rank:	-2				-2					-4.5

$T_+ = \Sigma(\text{positive ranks}) = 46.5$

$T_- = \Sigma(\text{negative ranks}) = 8.5$

$T = \text{smaller of } |T_+| \text{ or } |T_-| = 8.5$

$T_{.025(10)} = 8 < 8.5$ Do not reject H_0.

b. We cannot conclude that we have evidence supporting the hypothesis that there is a reliable increase in hypothesis generation and testing over time. (Here is a case in which alternative methods of breaking ties could lead to different conclusions.)

> Here we use the Matched-Pairs Signed-Ranks test because we are using the same 10 residents in each condition. It isn't really important, for choosing a test, whether these residents viewed the same or different videotape, but only that they are the same residents. The resident who gave an unusually high score early is likely to give at least a relatively high score later, and vice versa.

18.7 Independence of first-born children:

a. Analysis using Wilcoxon's matched-pairs signed-ranks test:

1st:	12	18	13	17	8	15	16	5	8	12
2nd:	10	12	15	13	9	12	13	8	10	8
Diff:	2	6	-2	4	-1	3	3	-3	-2	4
Rank:	4	17.5	4	11	1	8	8	8	4	11
Signed	4	17.5		11		8	8			11
Rank			-4		-1			-8	-4	

1st:	13	5	14	20	19	17	2	5	15	18
2nd:	8	9	8	10	14	11	7	7	13	12
Diff:	5	-4	6	10	5	6	-5	-2	2	6
Rank:	14	11	17.5	20	14	17.5	14	4	4	17.5
Signed	14		17.5	20	14	17.5			4	17.5
Rank:		-11					-14	-4		

$$T_+ = \Sigma R_+ = 164 \quad T_- = \Sigma R_- = 46 \quad T = 46$$

$$n = 20$$

$$T_{.025(20)} = 52 > 46$$

b. Reject H_0 and conclude that first-born children are more independent.

> Here is a good example of when we would use a "matched sample" test even though the same children do not perform in both conditions (nor could they). We are assuming that brothers and sisters are more similar to each other than they are to other children. Thus if the first born is particularly independent, we would guess that the second born has a higher than chance expectation of being more independent. This is because siblings share a common environment. Some parents raise very independent children, and others raise very dependent children.

18.9 Data in Exercise 18.7 plotted as a function of first-born's score:

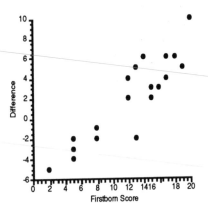

The scatter plot shows that the difference between the pairs is heavily dependent upon the score for the first born.

> This plot might suggest that the argument that I made for Exercise 18.7 may not be completely true. (Though it is certainly plausible on its face and does not invalidate the decision on the type of analysis.) If every second born child was exactly the same as every other second born child, then the difference within sibling pairs would depend entirely on the score of the first born child. And there would be no correlation between siblings. I would suggest plotting first born score against second born score to clarify what is going on.

18.11 The Wilcoxon matched-pairs signed-ranks test tests the null hypothesis that paired scores were drawn from identical populations or from symmetric populations with the same mean (and median). The corresponding t test tests the null hypothesis that the paired scores were drawn from populations with the same mean and assumes normality.

> This is an illustration of the argument that you buy things with assumptions. By making the more stringent assumptions of a *t* test, we buy greater specificity in our conclusions. However, if those assumptions are false, we may have used an inappropriate test.

18.13 Rejection of H_0 by a *t* test is a more specific statement than rejection using the appropriate distribution-free test because, by making assumptions about normality and homogeneity of variance, the *t* test refers specifically to population means.

18.15 Truancy and home situation of delinquent adolescents:

Analysis using Kruskal-Wallis one-way analysis of variance:

Natural Home		Foster Home		Group Home	
Score	Rank	Score	Rank	Score	Rank
15	18	16	19	10	9
18	22	14	16	13	13.5
19	24.5	20	26	14	16
14	16	22	27	11	10
5	4.5	19	24.5	7	6.5
8	8	5	4.5	3	2
12	11.5	17	20	4	3
13	13.5	18	22	18	22
7	6.5	12	11.5	2	1
$R_i =$ 124.5		170.5		83	

$N = 27$

$n = 9$

$$H = \frac{12}{N(N+1)} \sum \frac{R_i^2}{n_i} - 3(N+1)$$

$$= \frac{12}{27(27+1)} \left[\frac{124.5^2}{9} + \frac{170.5^2}{9} + \frac{83^2}{9} \right] - 3(27+1)$$

$$= 6.757 \quad [\chi^2_{.05(2)} = 5.99] \quad \text{Reject } H_0.$$

> The Kruskal-Wallis test is appropriate here because we have multiple independent groups of subjects.

18.17 The study in Exercise 18.16 has the advantage over the one in Exercise 18.15 in that it eliminates the influence of individual differences (differences in overall level of truancy from one person to another).

> Here we used Friedman's test because the same people were measured at different times, almost insuring that the observations would not be independent of one another.

18.19 For the data in Exercise 18.5:

a. Analyzed by chi-square:

	More	Fewer	Total
Observed	7	3	10
Expected	5	5	10

$$\chi^2 = \sum \frac{(O-E)^2}{E} = \frac{(7-5)^2}{5} + \frac{(3-5)^2}{5}$$

$$= 1.6 \quad [\chi^2_{.05(1)} = 3.84] \quad \text{Do not reject } H_0.$$

b. Analyzed by Friedman's test:

Before		After	
8	(2)	7	(1)
4	(1)	9	(2)
2	(1)	3	(2)
2	(1)	6	(2)
4	(2)	3	(1)
8	(1)	10	(2)
3	(1)	6	(2)
1	(1)	7	(2)
3	(1)	8	(2)
9	(2)	7	(1)
	(13)		(17)

$$N = 10 \quad k = 2$$

$$\chi^2_F = \frac{12}{Nk(k+1)} \sum R_i^2 - 3N(k+1)$$

$$= \frac{12}{10(2)(2+1)} \left[13^2 + 17^2 \right] - 3(10)(2+1)$$

$$= 1.6 \quad [\chi^2_{.05(1)} = 3.84] \quad \text{Do not reject } H_0.$$

These are exactly equivalent tests in this case.

> The two tests are equivalent here because there are only two levels of the independent variable. This would not be true with more than two levels.